Leaving Certificate
Home Economics Higher & Ordinary

Contents

Student Study Essentials

Exam Paper Analysis Chart iii
Guide to Better Grades vii
Map your Progress! xiv
Online Study Hub – visit **www.edco.ie/onlinestudyhub**

Completed (✓)

Higher Level

2024 State Examinations Commission Higher Level Paper 1	☐
2023 State Examinations Commission Higher Level Deferred Paper 20	☐
2023 State Examinations Commission Higher Level Paper 39	☐
2022 State Examinations Commission Higher Level Deferred Paper 58	☐
2022 State Examinations Commission Higher Level Paper 77	☐
2021 State Examinations Commission Higher Level Paper 95	☐
2020 State Examinations Commission Higher Level Paper 113	☐
2019 State Examinations Commission Higher Level Paper 129	☐
2018 State Examinations Commission Higher Level Paper 140	☐
2017 State Examinations Commission Higher Level Paper 151	☐
2016 State Examinations Commission Higher Level Paper 162	☐
2015 State Examinations Commission Higher Level Paper 173	☐

Ordinary Level

2024 State Examinations Commission Ordinary Level Paper 184	☐
2023 State Examinations Commission Ordinary Level Paper 203	☐
2022 State Examinations Commission Ordinary Level Paper 222	☐
2021 State Examinations Commission Ordinary Level Paper 240	☐

Continued

The Publisher has made every effort to trace and correctly acknowledge copyright holders. If, however, they have inadvertently overlooked any, they will be pleased to make the necessary arrangements at the first opportunity.

	Completed (✓)
2020 State Examinations Commission Ordinary Level Paper 258	☐
2019 State Examinations Commission Ordinary Level Paper 274	☐
2018 State Examinations Commission Ordinary Level Paper 285	☐
2017 State Examinations Commission Ordinary Level Paper 296	☐
2016 State Examinations Commission Ordinary Level Paper 307	☐

Student STUDY ESSENTIALS

	2012	2013	2014	2015	2016	2017	2018	2019	2020	2021	2022	2022 deferred paper	2023	2023 deferred paper	2024
Marriage				B5		B5					B5				
Marriage Breakdown						B5							B5		
Family as a Caring Unit	B5				B5									B5	B5
Generation Conflict							B5								
Roles and Responsibilities			B5						B5		B5				
Children	B5						B5								
Family Law		B5		B5			B5						B5		
Making a Will											B5				
Elective 1 – Home Design & Management															
Housing requirements		C1a			C1a	C1b	C1a							C1a	
Housing Styles		C1a			C1a			C1a	C1a	C1a		C1b	C1c	C1a	
Planning Permission					C1a					C1a					
Building standards							C1a								
Housing Provision		C1a	C1c			C1a			C1b					C1a	
Interior Design	C1c		C1b	C1a					C1a		C1a		C1a	C1b	C1a
Professional services											C1a				
Materials in the Home			C1a												
Environment & Energy Efficiency			C1a			C1a	C1b					C1c	C1c	C1c	C1b
Renewable energy			C1a				C1c				C1c				
Electricity & Gas				C1b				C1c						C1c	C1b
Water				C1c											
Heating	C1a				C1b				C1c			C1a	C1a		
Insulation			C1a								C1c	C1a			C1c
Ventilation	C1b			C1a		C1c					C1b				C1c
Lighting		C1b			C1c					C1b			C1b		
Water supply										C1c					
Flooring		C1c									C1a				
Walls								C1b							
Furniture						C1c									
Elective 2 – Textiles, Fashion & Design															
Design and garment construction											C2a		C2a	C2a	
Fashion design/ influences											C2c	C2a		C2c	C2a
Fabric production											C2b				C2b
Fashion Trends						C2a	C2a	C2a					C2c	C2c	C2c
Contemporary Fashion		C2a	C2a	C2a		C2b		C2a					C2c		
Textile Science	C2b	C2b		C2b	C2b	C2b	C2b	C2b	C2b		C2b	C2b	C2b	C2b	C2b
Design Evaluation		C2a	C2a											C2a	C2a
Garment Construction		C2c	C2b	C2b	C2b		C2b								
Commercial patterns												C2c			
Clothing & Textile Industries	C2a	C2c	C2c						C2c			C2c			
Fashion Design					C2c				C2a				C2a		
Irish Fashion Industry						C2c		C2c		C2c					C2c
Elective 3 – Social Studies															
Social Change & The Family			C3b									C3c	C3c		
Education		C3c	C3a	C3b	C3b		C3a	C3a	C3a		C3c	C3a		C3b	C3a
Childcare	C3c				C3b			C3b				C3c	C3a	C3c	
Child Development									C3a						
Work		C3a	C3c	C3a				C3a		C3b			C3a		
Work/life balance										C3c			C3a		
Leisure	C3b			C3c		C3c	C3c		C3c		C3b				C3c
Unemployment	C3a						C3a		C3b		C3a				C3b
Women							C3b							C3a	
Gender Roles						C3c	C3b							C3a	
Legislation								C3a							
Poverty		C3b				C3a		C3c		C3a		C3b	C3b		
Responses to Unemployment & Poverty	C3a														C3b
Emigration							C3b								
Volunteering								C3b							

Exceptional topics for 2023 HL deferred paper:
- Cheese
- Food Safety Authority of Ireland
- Retail Outlets
- Components of Management
- Marriage: Cultural Variations
- Marital Rights and Responsibilities

Exceptional topics for 2024 HL paper:
- Fats and Oils in the Diet
- Production of Margarine
- Choosing Household Textiles
- Household Technology
- Sensory Analysis Testing
- The Irish Food Industry

Home Economics at Leaving Certificate — Higher and Ordinary

Exam Paper Analysis Chart: Higher Level

	2012	2013	2014	2015	2016	2017	2018	2019	2020	2021	2022	2022 deferred paper	2023	2023 deferred paper
Food Science & Nutrition														
Protein			B1						B1					
Carbohydrates – Fibre	B1				B1	B1								B1
Lipids		B1					B1					B1		
Vitamins	B2				B2			B2		B1			B1	
Minerals			B1					B1Ca		B1			B1 (Fe)	
Diet & Health														
Food Choices							B1		B1				B3	B1
Meal planning										B1			B1	
Energy	B1													B1
Special Diets & Menus				B1		B1	B2		B1		B2			B2
Dietary Guidelines		B1			B1	B1	B1	B1			B1	B1		B2
Health and wellbeing										B1				
Dietary & Food Requirements	B1	B1	B1							B1				
Preparation & Processing														
The Irish Food Industry			B2									B2		
Meat			B2											
Fish					B2								B2	
Dairy														
Eggs			B2							B2		B3		
Cheese						B2								
Novel Protein Foods							B2			B2				
Cereals									B2					
Fruit & Veg	B2							B2						
Meal Management & Planning										B1	B1			B1
Sensory Analysis		B2			B3									
Preparation & Cooking			B3											
Food Labelling & Packaging		B1			B3		B1	B1			B1			B3
Food Processing & Profiles							B2		B2			B2	B3	
Food Preparation														
Food Additives							B3			B2		B3	B2	
Food Legislation									B3				B3	
Microbiology				B3				B3		B3				
Food Spoilage		B3						B3		B3				
Food Preservation	B3	B3	B2		B3				B3			B2	B3	
Food Safety & Hygiene	B3		B3							B3		B2	B2	
Resource Management & Consumer Studies														
Family Resource Management		B4								B4			B4	
Management Components		B4												
Household Finance/Budgeting	B4		B1	B4				B4						
Savings				B4										
Credit										B4				
Housing					B4					B4				
Mortgage						B4				B4				
Purchasing Process												B4		B4
Household Technology			B4			B4		B4						B4
Consumer Choices					B4								B4	
Retail Psychology													B4	
Consumer Protection					B4									B4
Consumer Legislation									B4	B4				
Consumer & Environment			B4				B4	B4						B4
The Family In Society														
Sociological Concepts		B5					B5					B5	B5	
The Family			B5	B5			B5				B5		B5	
Family Structures								B5		B5		B5		
Family Functions		B5							B5					

The following table has identified the areas of the exam paper where the specific topic is e.g B1 = Sec B question 1, B4 Question 4 and the elective is represented as C1 a, b, c (Home Design & Management), C2 a, b, c (Textile Fashion & Design), c (Social Studies), depending on which elective you have studied.

Exam Paper Analysis Chart: Ordinary Level

	2013	2014	2015	2016	2017	2018	2019	2020	2021	2022	2023	2024
Food Choice												B1
Food Science & Nutrition												
Protein	B1					B1					B1	
Carbohydrates		B1					B1					B1
Lipids				B1					B1			
Vitamins					B1							
Minerals			B1					B1		B1		
Water											B1	
Diet & Health												
Special Diets and Menus				B1		B1		B2				
Energy	B2							B2				
Menus		B1	B2					B2		B2		
Meal Planning											B1	B1
Healthy Eating Guidelines	B2	B1	B1	B2	B2	B2		B2				
Dietary & Food Requirements	B1											
The Irish Diet		B2										
Special Diets									B1			B2
Dietary guidelines									B2			
Preparation & Processing												
Buying food									B1			B1
The Irish Food Industry												B3
Meat					B3			B1			B2	
Fish			B3					B3				
Dairy		B2							B1	B1		
Cheese							B3					
Eggs				B3								
Cereals							B3			B2		
Fruit & Veg		B1		B2	B1				B3			B2
Preparation & Cooking			B3									
Food Safety & Hygiene											B3	
Soup		B3										
Processing & Packaging		B3		B3				B1	B3			B3
Food Spoilage												
Preservation											B3	
Resource Management & Consumer Studies												
Family Resource Management												
Household Budget				B4					B4			
Credit									B4			
Household Finance												
Online Shopping						B1						
Housing		B4					B4				B4	
Household Technology	B3		B4		B4			B4		B4	B3	
Purchasing												B4
Rights & Responsibilities	B4					B4				B4		
Consumer Responsibility								B4				
Consumer Protection			B4			B4						B4
Small claims court						B4						B4
Consumer & Environment	B4	B4								B4	B4	
Environment							B4					
Savings			B4									
Insurance							B4				B4	
The Family In Society												
The Family					B5							
Family Structures	B5								B5			
Family Functions		B5					B5					B5
Family Relationship		B5										B5
Responsibilities of adolescents									B5			
The Elderly	B5					B5					B5	
Marriage		B5		B5				B5		B5		
Marriage Break Down								B5		B5		

Student STUDY ESSENTIALS

	2013	2014	2015	2016	2017	2018	2019	2020	2021	2022	2023	2024
Generational Conflict						B5	B5				B5	
Gender Roles		B5										
Family Law												
Making a Will						B5					B5	
Children's Needs & Rights												
Elective 1 – Home Design & Management												
House Building + Design			C1a				C1a					C1b
Housing Styles							C1a					
Housing Provision			C1b		C1c	C1a				C1b		
Buying a house									C1b			
Housing Requirements									C1b			
Floor Plan								C1a		C1a		
Planning Permission							C1a					C1b
Local amenities						C1b						
Interior design				C1a	C1b			C1a	C1c		C1a	
Furniture			C1b			C1c						
Environment & Energy Efficiency				C1a						C1b	C1b	
Electricity & Gas		C1a			C1c					C1c	C1a	
Water			C1c			C1a			C1a		C1c	C1a
Solar energy									C1a			
Heating				C1a			C1c				C1a	
Insulation	C1a				C1a				C1a			
Ventilation									C1b			C1c
Lighting		C1c					C1b			C1a		
Flooring	C1b			C1b								
Wall Finishes	C1b								C1c			
Elective 2 – Textiles, Fashion & Design												
Contemporary Fashion						C2a	C2a					C2c
Fashion Design							C2a					C2a
Children Clothing								C2a				
Fashion Trends								C2b		C2a	C2a	C2c
Textile Science	C2c	C2c	C2b	C2b	C2b		C2b				C2b	C2b
Occasion wear									C2a			
Fibre/fabric construction									C2b	C2b		C2b
Design Evaluation	C2b	C2a	C2a	C2a							C2a	C2a
Garment Construction		C2c	C2c	C2b		C2b						
Clothing & Textile Industries		C2b							C2c			
Footwear				C2c								
Clothing influence									C2c	C2c		C2c
Irish clothing industry		C2b				C2c					C2c	
Elective 3 – Social Studies												
Social Change & The Family												C3c
Education	C3a			C3a			C3a	C3a		C3a	C3a, C3b	C3c
Childcare			C3c		C3c			C3b		C3c		
Work	C3c	C3a	C3b	C3a	C3b				C3a		C3c	C3a
Family & Work									C3c			C3a
Leisure		C3b	C3b	C3c			C3b		C3b			C3b
Unemployment	C3b					C3a			C3c		C3a	
Poverty	C3b	C3c				C3a		C3c		C3a		
Migration							C3c			C3b		
Responses to Employment & Poverty		C3c										
Women		C3a				C3b					C3c	C3a
Employment legislation				C3a								
Adult Education				C3b								

Exceptional topics for 2024 OL paper:

- Milk and Dairy Products
- Milk Processing
- Conditions for a Valid Marriage
- Choosing Household Technology
- Electrical Safety
- Responsibilities of a Married Couple

Home Economics at Leaving Certificate
Guide to Better Grades — Higher and Ordinary Levels

Structure of the Paper

This examination will be a written terminal examination. The examination is to be marked out of 320 marks (or 280 marks for those candidates taking the Textiles, Fashion and Design Elective). The examination paper will be presented at two levels: Ordinary and Higher.

For students who choose elective 1 (Home Design and Management) or elective 3 (Social Studies) the written examination is worth 80% of the marks and the Food Studies Coursework is worth 20% of the marks. For students who choose the Textile, Fashion and Design elective, the written examination is worth 70% of the marks, the Food Studies Coursework is worth 20% of the marks and the Textile Fashion and Design course work is worth 10% of the overall mark.

The written examination will be worth 80% of the final examination mark (or 70% for those candidates taking the Textiles, Fashion and Design Elective).

Time – 2 1/2 hours

15 minutes to read the paper carefully and select the questions to be attempted.

Three Sections

Section A

Short Answer questions ✓ **60 marks**

- Covering the Food Studies and Resource Management and Consumer Studies core aspects of the course.
- Candidates will be expected to answer ten questions from a choice of fourteen. Each question will carry 6 marks. Questions should be answered in the space provided in the paper. Remember to return the short questions with your answer book.
- Spend **25 mins** on this section. It will be to your benefit if your answers are presented clearly.

Section B

Long Answer questions ✓ **180 marks**

- Covering all sections of the core. Candidates will be expected to answer three questions. **Question 1 (80 marks)** will be compulsory and will be based on the Food Studies, Social Studies and Resource Management and Consumer Studies sections of the core.
- Spend **35 mins** on question 1 which is a compulsory question.
- **Questions 2, 3, 4 and 5 (50 marks each)**. Candidates will be required to answer **two out of the four questions**. The questions will be based on the core and may involve integration of more than one area.
- Spend **20 mins** on each 50 mark question chosen.
- These questions should be answered in the answer book provided.

Section C

The Elective ✓ **(80 marks/40 marks)**

- There will be three elective questions, one for each elective. **Questions 1 and 3** are worth **80 marks each. Question 2** is worth **40 marks.** Candidates will be required to answer just **one of these questions.** Within each question there will be three parts. **Part A** will be compulsory **(50 marks/25 marks)**. There will be a choice between **Part B** and **Part C (30 and 15 marks)**.
- Spend **35 mins** on this section.
- In this section candidates will have the option to answer the elective question 1 or 2 or 3 (Elective 2, which is the textile question, is worth 40 marks). There is a fourth question provided based on the Core topics. This question is to be answered **instead** of an elective question and is worth 80 marks.

Using your Time Wisely

During your preparation for this exam you should try to stick to the suggested times for answering each of the different types of questions, e.g.

- **Reading time** – 15 mins.
- **Short Answer Questions** – 25 mins.
- **Long Answer Compulsory Question** – 35 mins.
- **Long Answer Questions 2, 3, 4** and **5** – 20 mins for each of the two questions you have chosen.
- **Elective** – 35 mins.

If you work too slowly, you will not complete all of the questions, or you might have to rush towards the end. Either way you will not do your best. Remember, the questions you answer last may be the ones you are least sure of and will therefore take more time to answer. If you work too quickly, you are probably not giving yourself enough time and you could lose marks. In an ideal situation you should finish your paper only a minute or two before the end of the examination.

Completing all Parts of the Question

Sometimes examiners see that a candidate has missed parts of the examination paper. It is not unknown for candidates to turn over two pages accidentally or to fail to turn over the last page on the paper. Check before you finish that you have not missed any questions.

If you find a question, or part of a question, difficult you might want to leave it and come back later. If you do this, do not forget to go back. Don't be afraid to make a guess or put down something you are not sure about. There are no penalties for wrong answers. You just score marks for the things you have right.

Reading the Question Correctly

Some questions provide a great deal of information. This may be in the form of text, in diagrams, in graphs or in tables. This information is for you to use or process as part of your answer. Very often it is clear from the answers of the candidates that they have not read the question and all of the information given. If you find you are writing your answer without using the information given, check that you are answering all of the question being asked.

There is a tendency for candidates to write answers to questions they have answered before, perhaps in a previous preparation exam, rather than the one set.

Some candidates take a highlighter pen into the examination and after they have read the questions they go through them again and highlight the important words.

Points to Note

- Sketch your answers in your answerbook not on the paper.
- Underline the key words in the question.
- Take note of the mark allocation for different parts of the question, as it is usually an indication of how many points of information needed.
- Label diagrams carefully when requested to do so.
- Do not go overboard on the time allocation per question.
- Answer the question you are being asked not the one you would like to be asked.

Understanding the Command Words

- **List** – Set out the points; they do not have to be explained in detail.
- **Enumerate** – Points must be made in order of importance and a brief explanation of each one must be given.
- **Principle** – Give a reason or a description of the working method.
- **Discuss** – Give two sides of the argument. This is important in sociology questions.
- **Characteristics** – List the qualities.
- **Properties** – List the attributes of a substance.
- **Opinion** – Give a reasoned answer.
- **Compare** – Show likeness; use a table if possible.

As Home Economics is a multi-disciplinary subject, it is recommended that it be studied within a framework that integrates the related elements and processes within the core and the selected elective. It follows, therefore, that assessment questions and tasks will promote this principle of integration.

The key point in answering Home Economics questions is to link as many areas of the course as possible. For example, if you learn from the theory of fats and oils, you must also learn lipids, pastry and cake mixtures.

Revising

Remember Home Economics is a multi-disciplinary subject you should therefore be able to integrate different aspects of the course in your answers to questions e.g. food processing and the freezer, family resource management and meal planning are just some examples you may come across in the course.

It is a good idea when you are revising to keep notes and provide link ups for various topics.

Answering Questions

To gain full marks:

- Read the question carefully.
- Write a brief plan of the question.
- Note the specific requirements of each question, e.g. nutritive value of fish, the functions of the family.
- Each question will show the amount of marks allocated, e.g.
  – Outline the protection provided to the consumer by the Hire Purchase Act 1960. (8)
  – State one property of water. (2)

In the exam you will earn full marks if accurate and detailed information is given, ¾ marks if limited detail but generally accurate information is given, ½ marks if answer is lacking detail/very basic information given or less than ½ marks if inaccurate or irrelevant information is written. Avoid writing irrelevant information and use the appropriate vocabulary, e.g. sociology, scientific term.

Sample Exam Answers Higher Level 2023

In section B you are required to answer Question 1 (80 marks) and any other two questions from this section. Below are some sample answers from Section B.

Section B

Answer Question 1 and any other two questions from this section.

Question 1 is worth 80 marks. Questions 2, 3, 4 and 5 are worth 50 marks each.

Question 1

'Adequate micronutrient intake during the teenage years is important for optimum growth and development.' *(National Teen Food Survey II Report 2021 adapted from iuna.net)*

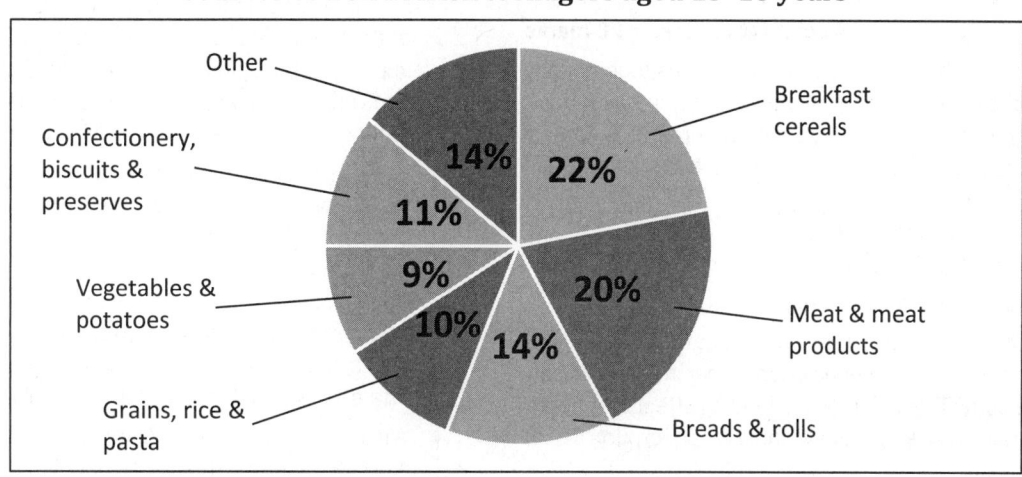

Sources of iron in Irish teenagers aged 13–18 years

a) Using the information provided in the chart, comment and elaborate on the importance of including different sources of iron in a teenagers' diet. Refer to four sources in your answer.

4 points @ 5 marks = 20 marks

Comment

Twenty-two per cent of an Irish teenager's iron intake is obtained from breakfast cereals. Breakfast cereals are the greatest contributor of iron in the diet of Irish teenagers.

Elaborate

Many breakfast cereals are naturally high in non-haem iron, for example porridge oats. This non-haem iron can be easily converted to haem iron through the inclusion of vitamin C as part of their breakfast, for example, including a glass of orange juice or a fruit smoothie. Other common ingredients included in breakfast cereals include dried fruits and nuts (e.g. in muesli or granola), which also contribute to non-haem iron intake. Many refined breakfast cereals are fortified with iron during processing.

Comment

Twenty per cent of an Irish teenager's iron intake is obtained from meat and meat products. Meat and meat products are the second greatest contributor of iron in the diet of Irish teenagers.

Elaborate

Red meat and meat products (including offal) are an excellent source of haem iron in the diet of teenagers. This is particularly important in the diet of teenage girls who experience iron loss because of menstruation. These foods also have the additional benefit of being high in HBV protein which is essential for growth and repair in this rapid period of development. Meat and meat products form a large part of a teenager's diet, for example, having a chicken salad sandwich for lunch, or beef lasagne for dinner. This widespread use of meat and meat products across the diet has resulted in the high contribution of iron.

Comment

Ten per cent of an Irish teenager's iron intake is obtained from grains, rice and pasta. Grains, rice and pasta are the second lowest contributor of iron in the diet of Irish teenagers.

Elaborate

Wholegrain varieties of grains, rice and pasta are a good source of non-haem iron in the diet; however, the high-fibre content of these foods can negatively impact and prevent iron absorption. This is an issue for teenagers to be aware of. These foods are quick and easy to incorporate into the diet (e.g. rice cakes, wholemeal crackers), making them a convenient option on a day-to-day basis. While some teenagers (e.g. those involved in sports and athletics) will benefit from the non-haem iron provided by these high-energy foods, others may choose to reduce their intake due to their high-calorie content, particularly those who are less active. This may be the reason for the overall low contribution that these foods make to iron intake.

Comment

Nine per cent of an Irish teenager's iron intake is obtained from vegetables and potatoes. Vegetables and potatoes are the lowest contributor of iron in the diet of Irish teenagers.

ix

Student STUDY ESSENTIALS

Elaborate

Some classes of vegetables are good sources of non-haem iron, namely pulses (e.g. beans, peas and lentils) and leafy greens (e.g. cabbage, broccoli and kale). These foods are readily available and very versatile (e.g. having a salad for lunch or having a vegetable side at dinner). However, many teenagers neglect their intake of vegetables during these years and fail to achieve their intake of 5–7 portions per day, citing lack of flavour and taste as the main reason for their dislike. This may be the reason why this food group contributes so little to iron intake.

b) Identify and elaborate on the factors that affect the absorption of iron in the body.

4 points @ 5 marks = 20 marks

- Consuming haem and non-haem sources together as part of a meal can increase the rate of non-haem iron absorption. For example, serving bacon (haem iron) with cabbage (non-haem iron) for an evening meal.
- Ensuring that meals contain a source of Vitamin C will assist in the conversion of non-haem iron to haem iron. For example, having a glass of orange juice with a breakfast of scrambled eggs on wholemeal toast.
- Excess fibre in the diet, i.e. having above the recommended 35g per day, can hinder iron absorption in the body. This is due to the binding effect that fibre has on iron, making it unavailable for absorption.
- An excessive intake of tannins (plant-based compounds found in tea and coffee) can also hinder iron absorption.

c) Give an account of Vitamin C with reference to:
   - **Biological function**
   - **Effects of deficiency**
   - **Properties**

Biological functions

4 points @ 3 marks = 12 marks

- Vitamin C is needed to maintain healthy gums and prevent the onset of gum diseases such as scurvy.
- Vitamin C assists in the healing of wounds, helping to speed up healing time and reduce the risk of infection.
- Vitamin C works as an antioxidant, protecting against free radicals, reducing the risk of cancers and heart disease.
- Vitamin C helps to boost the body's immune system by helping white blood cells fight infection and illness.

Effects of deficiency

2 points @ 2 marks = 4 marks

- As less connective tissue is made, this can lead to an increase in bleeding and bruising in the body.
- Due to a reduced absorption of iron and subsequent lack of haemoglobin in the body, anaemia can occur, resulting in fatigue, dizziness and overall lack of energy.

Properties

2 points @ 2 marks = 4 marks

- Vitamin C is easily destroyed by heat; for example, the natural vitamin C reserves are lost when milk is pasteurised.
- Vitamin C is easily destroyed by metals, for example, when Vitamin C rich foods such as vegetables are cooked in copper pans.

d) Discuss the guidelines a family should follow, when doing their weekly shopping on a restricted budget, in order to provide for their nutritional needs.

5 points @ 4 marks = 20 marks

- Families should plan meals around foods that are currently in season, e.g. potatoes in summer. Not only are they fresher and at their most nutritious, but the large supply, which can adequately meet consumer demand, also means that prices will be cheaper.
- Families can select own-brand goods instead of the market leader, for example, choosing the supermarket's own-brand milk instead of the branded equivalent. In most cases, the nutritional value will not differ significantly and huge savings can be made.
- Families should avail of special offers where possible, for example, 'Buy One Get One Free', or '3 for the price of 2' offers. This is a useful way of making the family's budget go further, especially when purchasing non-perishable foods, e.g. pasta and rice, which have a long shelf life. If the family has sufficient freezer space, this can also be useful when availing of special offers on perishable foods, e.g. fresh meats.
- When choosing protein-based foods such as meat, cheaper, tougher cuts can be bought to reduce expenditure. Although careful planning regarding the method of cookery will be needed, the family will not have to compromise on nutritional value, especially in terms of HBV protein and iron.
- Families should try to plan weekly meals in advance of completing their weekly shop and make a shopping list based on this. In doing so, the risk of buying unnecessary, impulse purchases will be reduced. Not only will this help to restrict spending, it will also prevent unnecessary food waste if the food is not used.

Question 2

'Nutritional experts recommend consuming 2–3 portions of fish each week for a balanced diet.'

(www.goodfoodireland.ie)

a) Discuss the nutritional significance of fish in the diet.

5 points @ 4 marks = 20 marks

- Fish is a good source of high biological value, with a protein content of 16–18%. The biological value of fish is approximately 80 to 90%, meaning that it is an excellent source of the essential amino acid. Fish is an easily digested source of protein, making it useful in the diets of the elderly during periods of cell growth and repair or people recovering from injuries.
- The fat content of fish varies, depending on type. Oily fish contains approximately 15% polyunsaturated fat, and contributes to the intake of both omega-3 and -6 fatty acids. These fatty acids are beneficial for both heart health and brain development. White fish is almost deficient in fat, with an approximate content of 0.5%. This is due to the removal of the liver during

- the processing of white fish, where much of the fat is stored. As a result, white fish is useful in low-fat and low-kilo-calorie diets.
- Fish is lacking in carbohydrate (0%) as a result of glycogen depletion upon the struggle experienced after being caught. To make up for this loss, fish is usually served with a carbohydrate-rich food, e.g. fish pie with creamy mashed potato.
- Vitamins account for approximately 1–2% of the nutritional value. B-group vitamins, which are essential for energy release from food and a healthy nervous system, are found in both white and oily fish. Vitamins A (essential for healthy eyesight) and D (essential for calcium absorption) are found in oily fish. Oysters provide a source of vitamin C.
- Minerals account for approximately 1–2% of the nutritional value of fish. Fish provides useful amounts of zinc (function), potassium (function) and phosphorus (function). Shellfish are a good source of non-haem iron, while tinned fish, e.g. sardines or mackerel, contribute to calcium intake.

b) **Give a detailed account of one process used to extend the shelf life of fish.**

Refer to:
- Name
- Underlying principle
- Effects

Name   1 point @ 3 marks = 3 marks

Canning

Underlying principle

3 points @ 3 marks = 9 marks

- The canning process involves the use of very high temperatures (up to 140°C) to destroy any microorganism or enzyme present.
- The processed fish is then stored in sterile cans to avoid the re-introduction of micro-organisms.
- The cans are sealed to prevent the re-entry of micro-organisms, while also acting as a barrier against oxygen.

Effects   2 points @ 3 marks = 6 marks

- The calorie content of the fish can be increased depending on how it is canned, e.g. the canning of tuna in oil will increase the calorie content from fat.
- Vitamin B_1 is destroyed due to the high temperatures used in the canning process.

c) **Describe the role of the Food Safety Authority of Ireland (FSAI) in the food industry.**

2 points @ 6 marks = 12 marks

- The FSAI works to enforce food safety legislation through different agencies, e.g. the HSE, while also providing advice on food safety issues to other bodies, e.g. to government ministers (e.g. the Minister for Agriculture), the food industry and consumers in general.
- The FSAI enforces food safety standards through the use of HSE-appointed Environmental Health Officers (EHOs). If a food business is in breach of food safety legislation, the FSAI can do the following:
  - Issue an improvement notice (if there is likely to be a threat to public health, the food business must make the recommended improvements).
  - Issue a closure order (if the food business is likely to pose a serious threat to public health).
  - Issue a prohibition order (if the risk to public health is from a particular product or item of food). This prohibits the sale of this product either temporarily or permanently.

Question 3

'People are becoming more experimental in their culinary choices.' *(www.bordbia.ie)*

a) **Discuss the choices that affect food choices for families today.**

3 points @ 4 marks = 12 marks

Culture

The country in which we live influences our family's food choices, i.e. most countries have a staple food within their diet (a food that is plentiful and forms the main part of the diet in a country). For example, potatoes in Ireland, rice in China, pasta in Italy, etc. Some religions have rules regarding food choices, e.g. Muslims do not eat pork, Buddhists tend to be vegan or vegetarian. In Ireland, many Catholics still abstain from meat on Ash Wednesday and Good Friday.

Availability

Not all foods are available all year round, i.e. some foods are seasonal. For example, Brussels sprouts at Christmas or strawberries in the summer. As a result of the advances in technology and transportation, more and more foods are now readily available throughout the year, i.e. canned strawberries and frozen Brussels sprouts. Some people may have limited access to foods, e.g. those living in very rural or remote areas of the country.

Nutritional awareness

People are now more health conscious and are more aware of the nutritional value of food and therefore, tend to make better food choices. This awareness is due to the work of groups such as the Health Promotion Unit and Bord Bia, and subjects such as Home Economics, SPHE and Science. Many food companies now place specific information regarding nutritional value on the front of their products to make it easier for consumers to make healthy choices.

b) **Profile an added-value food you have studied.**

Refer to:
- Name
- Stages of production
- Packaging and labelling

Name   1 point @ 2 marks = 2 marks
Cheese

Stages of production

           6 points @ 3 marks = 18 marks

- First of all, the milk is pasteurised to destroy pathogenic bacteria present, after which lactic acid bacteria (LAB) is added to the milk. The addition of LAB converts the lactose in the milk to lactic acid, which will help to both flavour and preserve the finished cheese.
- Next, the milk is heated to 30°C and rennet is added. Rennet contains an enzyme called rennin, which separates the milk into curds and whey. This can take between 30 and 45 minutes.
- Once fully separate, the whey is drained off and the curd is chopped. The curd is then heated to 40°C to release and drain off more excess whey. This is known as scalding.
- At this point the curds are cut into blocks and are piled on top of each other to help drain away even more whey. This is known as cheddaring.
- The curd is cut once more, and 2% salt is added, which will help to both preserve and enhance the flavour of the finished cheese.
- The salted curd is pressed into moulds and left for varying amounts of time. The moulds are sprayed with hot water to form a protective rind on the cheese. The cheese is then left to ripen for 3–12 months.

Packaging and labelling

           2 points @ 3 marks = 6 marks

- The finished cheese is packaged using a variety of materials such as resealable polythene bags, waxed paper, aluminium foil and plastic tubs.
- Finally, the cheese is labelled and will include the following information: type of cheese, e.g. mature Cheddar; brand, e.g. Charleville; quantity, e.g. 100g; nutritional information; date stamp.

c) **Name and describe the role of one physical conditioning agent used in food processing.**

     Name = 1 point @ 4 marks = 4 marks
     Role = 2 points @ 4 marks = 8 marks

Polyphosphates (anti-caking agents)

- Anti-caking agents, such as magnesium carbonate, are used to prevent lumping in dried foods.
- Common foods that make use of anti-caking agents include cake mixes, e.g. Betty Crocker, chocolate milk powder and table salt.

Question 4

'Customers must be constantly vigilant to protect themselves.' (www.thacai.ie)

a) Discuss how the following factors affect management in the home:
- Stages in the lifecycle of the family
- Employment patterns
- Values

           4 points @ 5 marks = 20 marks

(one point on each factor plus one other)

Stages in the lifecycle of the family

- The arrival of children can put pressure on family resources such as time, energy and money. One spouse may make the decision to leave the workforce and become a full-time stay-at-home parent if it means being better able to care for the needs and wants of the family.
- As children grow up, their needs, wants and priorities change. Providing for basic essential needs, e.g. food and clothing, can put extra financial pressure on families, which in turn can result in both parents going out to work. This can make managing household tasks such as home maintenance, cooking and cleaning more difficult to achieve due to decreased time spent at home.

Employment patterns

- The number of parents working outside the home, and the type of work undertaken, e.g. full-time or part-time, will influence the management of the home. Dual-income families may have greater access to material resources, e.g. goods, services, equipment due to a higher income, but may lack the necessary time and energy needed to achieve family goals.

Values

- Values and standards will influence the decisions made by a family. For example, a family that values the importance of caring for the environment will make more informed eco-friendly decisions regarding waste disposal. They might make greater efforts to recycle or compost where possible or avoid single-use plastics.

b) **Analyse how different techniques used by retailers influence consumer spending.**

           4 points @ 5 marks = 20 marks

(max of 2 points under each technique)

Shop layout and design

Wide aisles and a grid layout mean that consumers follow the flow of the aisles and ultimately see more products. Shops will regularly change the layout of the store. This causes the consumer to have to search more for items, which will result in a greater chance of impulse buying of other products.

In-store stimuli

The use of soft background music and low-level lighting makes the consumer feel relaxed and at ease, encouraging them to browse longer. The smell and aromas of freshly baked bread and cakes is also used to attract consumers into the store.

Product placement

Everyday essentials such as bread and milk are usually placed at the back of the store. This means that the consumer will have to pass other items, which they will hopefully pick up along the way.

Shelf position

Luxury, branded items are usually placed at eye-level, meaning they are in the line of sight of a consumer. Cheaper or own-brand versions of these products are placed up high or down low on the shelves, making them less apparent to the consumer.

c) **Describe how the responsibilities of a consumer can assist them in making wise choices.**

   2 points @ 5 marks = 10 marks

- Consumers have a responsibility to seek honest and truthful information so as to make well-thought-out and informed decisions. This ensures that consumers choose wisely and avoid making impulse decisions when selecting goods and services, for example, reviewing a number of options when buying a family car.
- Consumers have a responsibility to understand the balance between cost and quality. Consumers should understand that, in general, low cost can often mean low quality. When selecting goods and services, the desired level of quality required will most likely be reflected in the cost. For example, a tradesperson who is extremely cheap may not provide the best-quality service.

Question 5

The family is an integral social institution in society.

a) **Discuss the changes that have taken place in the family from the middle of the twentieth century to the present day.**

   5 points @ 4 marks = 20 marks

Middle of the twentieth century

- The urban-based nuclear family began to emerge as family members moved from rural areas in search of employment. This resulted in a decrease in the classic extended family of the early twentieth century.
- Families were smaller, usually with 4–6 children being the average. This occurred due to the decreased influence of the Church and the availability of contraception and information on family planning.
- The rights of women had improved, and they now had more say on parenting, finances and discipline. However, role segregation still existed, with women still being expected to remain in the home, while men went out to work.

Present day

- The nuclear family is the main family type today. However, there has also been an increase in the number of one-parent and blended families, mainly due to the introduction of separation and divorce.
- Most families today are egalitarian, with both parents having equal say on parenting, finances and discipline. Household tasks are equally shared and both parents may work outside of the home, i.e. a dual-income household.

b) **Explain the following sociological terms:**
   - **Universality of the family**
   - **Kinship**
   - **Monogamy**

   3 points @ 5 marks = 15 marks

Universality of the family

This refers to how the family is a universally known concept that is understood by all societies, regardless of the fact that the form that the family takes may change from one society to another.

Kinship

This refers to family links or relationships that are based on blood, marriage, common ancestry or other family ties such as adoption.

Monogamy

This refers to relationships/marriages where individuals have one, and only one, partner at a time. This is widely practised in Western society, for example in Ireland. The opposite is polygamy, which allows an individual to have more than one partner at any given time.

c) **Describe one legal option available in Ireland to couples when their marriage has broken down.**

   Name = 1 point @ 3 marks = 3 marks

   Description = 3 points @ 4 marks = 12 marks

Decree of divorce

- A decree of divorce is obtained when spouses wish to end an existing legal marriage to marry another partner.
- An application can be made to the court for a decree of divorce when the separating spouses have lived apart for at least two of the previous three years, with no reasonable prospect of reconciliation.
- The court must be satisfied that adequate provision and supports have been made for any dependent spouse and/or children before the decree is granted.

All rights reserved. No part of the Student Study Essentials and Edco Sample Papers may be reproduced, stored in a retrieval system, or transmitted in any form or by any means, electronic, mechanical, photocopying, recording or otherwise, without either the prior permission of the Publisher or a licence permitting restricted copying in Ireland issued by the Irish Copyright Licensing Agency, 63 Patrick Street, Dún Laoghaire, Co. Dublin.

Map Your Progress!

Tick each question as you complete it and again once you have finished an entire exam paper.

LEAVING CERTIFICATE HOME ECONOMICS (SCIENTIFIC & SOCIAL)	TIME	2024	2023 deferred paper	2023	2022 deferred paper	2022	2021	2020	2019	2018	2017	2016	2015
HIGHER LEVEL Entire Paper (200/240 marks)	**2 hrs 30 mins**												
Read over paper & select which questions to attempt	*15 mins*												
Section A – Short Answer Questions (30 marks – 6 marks per question) *Answer **5** out of 14*	25 mins												
Section B – Long Answer Questions (130 marks) *Answer **3** questions: Question **1** (80 marks) and **any 1** (50 marks each) out of Questions 2, 3, 4 and 5:*	35 mins for Q1 & 20 mins each for other 2 questions												
Question 1 *Compulsory													
Question 2													
Question 3													
Question 4													
Question 5													
Section C – The Elective *Answer **1** elective question:*	35 mins												
Elective 1 (80 marks) – Home Design & Management *Answer 1(a) & either 1(b) or 1(c)*													
Elective 2 (40 marks) – Textiles, Fashion & Design *Answer 2(a) & either 2(b) or 2(c)*													
Elective 3 (80 marks) – Social Studies *Answer 3(a) & either 3(b) or 3(c)*													
Question 4 (80 marks) – Core question *Answer 4(a) & either 4(b) or 4(c)*													
Exam Complete													

(Continued)

Map Your Progress!

LEAVING CERTIFICATE HOME ECONOMICS (SCIENTIFIC & SOCIAL)	TIME	2024	2023	2022	2021	2020	2019	2018	2017	2016
ORDINARY LEVEL Entire Paper (200/240 marks)	**2 hrs 30 mins**									
Read over paper & select which questions to attempt	15 mins									
Section A – Short Answer Questions (30 marks – 6 marks per question) *Answer **5** out of 14	25 mins									
Section B – Long Answer Questions (130 marks) *Answer **3** questions: Question **1** (80 marks) and **any 1** (50 marks each) out of Questions 2, 3, 4 and 5:	35 mins for Q1 & 20 mins each for other 2 questions									
Question 1 *Compulsory										
Question 2										
Question 3										
Question 4										
Question 5										

(Continued)

Map Your Progress!

LEAVING CERTIFICATE HOME ECONOMICS (SCIENTIFIC & SOCIAL)	TIME	2016	2017	2018	2019	2020	2021	2022	2023	2024
ORDINARY LEVEL Entire Paper (200/240 marks)	**2 hrs 30 mins**									
Section C – The Elective *Answer 1 elective question:	35 mins									
Elective 1 (80 marks) – Home Design & Management *Answer 1(a) & either 1(b) or 1(c)										
Elective 2 (40 marks) – Textiles, Fashion & Design *Answer 2(a) & either 2(b) or 2(c)										
Elective 3 (80 marks) – Social Studies *Answer 3(a) & either 3(b) or 3(c)										
Question 4 (80 marks) – Core question *Answer 4(a) & either 4(b) or 4(c)										
Exam Complete										

Leaving Cert Grades & CAO Points Calculation Chart

Higher				Ordinary		
% marks	Grade	Points		% marks	Grade	Points
90–100	H1	100		90–100	O1	56
80 < 90	H2	88		80 < 90	O2	46
70 < 80	H3	77		70 < 80	O3	37
60 < 70	H4	66		60 < 70	O4	28
50 < 60	H5	56		50 < 60	O5	20
40 < 50	H6	46		40 < 50	O6	12
30 < 40	H7	37		30 < 40	O7	0
0 < 30	H8	0		0 < 30	O8	0

Source: State Examinations Commission, 2010 & CAO, 2024.

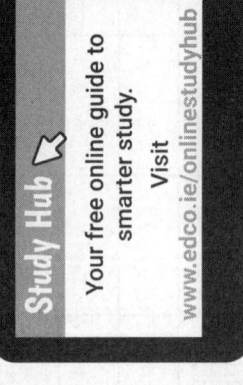

Study Hub
Your free online guide to smarter study.
Visit
www.edco.ie/onlinestudyhub

Remember

- Questions from Sections B and C should be answered in the answer book provided. Remember to return the short questions with your answer book.
- If you submitted Textiles, Fashion and Design coursework for examination, you may only attempt Question 2 in Section C.
- Label diagrams carefully when requested to do so.
- Take note of the mark allocations for different parts of the question, as it is usually an indication of how many points of information are needed.

Student Study Essentials © The Educational Company of Ireland, 2024

2024.M48

Coimisiún na Scrúduithe Stáit
State Examinations Commission

Leaving Certificate Examination 2024
Home Economics - Scientific and Social
Section A and Answerbook
Higher Level
Wednesday 5 June   Afternoon 2:00 - 4:30
280 or 320 marks

Examination Number

Date of Birth

For example, 3rd February 2005 is entered as 03 02 05

Centre Stamp

Instructions

Write your Examination Number and your Date of Birth in the boxes on the front cover.

Write your answers to all parts of the examination into this answerbook. This answerbook will be scanned and your work will be presented to an examiner on screen. Anything that you write outside of the answer areas may not be seen by the examiner.

Write your answers in blue or black pen. You may use pencil for sketches, graphs and diagrams only.

There are three sections in this examination. Questions for **Sections B and C** are supplied separately but your answers must be written in this answerbook.

Section A	60 marks
	Answer any **ten** questions in this section.
	Each question carries 6 marks.
Section B	180 marks
	Answer **Question 1** and any other **two** questions from this section.
	Question 1 is worth 80 marks.
	Questions 2, 3, 4 and 5 are worth 50 marks each.
Section C	40 or 80 marks
	Answer **one** elective question **or** Question 4 (core) to include **part (a)** and either **part (b) or part (c)**.
	If you submitted *Textiles, Fashion and Design* coursework for examination, you may only attempt Question 2 from this section.
	Electives 1 and 3 are worth 80 marks each.
	Elective 2 is worth 40 marks.
	Question 4 (core) is worth 80 marks.

Leaving Certificate Examination 2024
Home Economics – Higher level
Section A and answerbook

Section A 60 marks

Answer any **ten** questions from this section.
Each question carries 6 marks.
Write your answers in the spaces provided.

1. In relation to protein, explain deamination.

   Excess amino acids are broken down in the liver. The amino group is converted to ammonia then to urea broken down by the kidney produced a waste product in urine. Carboxyl group oxidised to produce heat & energy

2. State **two** biological functions of Vitamin A.

   (i) Produces rhodospin which aids eyes to see in dark light
   (ii) Growth in children

   Identify **two** dietary sources of Vitamin A.

   (i) Red peppers
   (ii) Carrots

3. Describe the following forms of iron and give **one** food source of each.

Form of iron	Description	Food source
Haem iron	Ferrous iron is easily absorbed. Mainly in animal sources	Red meat
Non-haem iron	Ferric iron is not easily absorbed, has to be changed into ferrous. Mainly in plant sources	Spinach

Leaving Certificate Examination 2024
Home Economics – Higher level
Section A and answerbook

4. Outline **two** meal planning guidelines that should be considered when planning meals for a person with osteoporosis.

(i) High in calcium, using foods such as milk, cheese & yoghurt, as calcium provides healthy bones & teeth

(ii) Foods high in Vitamin D such as oily fish eg tuna as it aids in the absorption of calcium

5. Complete the table below in relation to alternative (novel) protein foods.

	Source	Product
Plant	Soya beans	TVP
Micro-organisms	Fustrium venturn	Quorn

6. Explain the role of **each** of the following in the production of cheese.

Lactic acid bacteria	This starter culture changes lactose into lactic acid, which coagulates the milk improving flavour and acts as a preservative
Rennet	Contains the enzyme rennin which changes caseygin into caesin, separates the milk into curds & wheys

Leaving Certificate Examination 2024
Home Economics – Higher level
Section A and answerbook

7. Identify **two** contaminants that can enter the food chain. State **one** possible source and **one** possible effect on the body of each contaminant named.

Contaminant	Source	Effect on the body
(i)		
(ii)		

8. Differentiate between **each** of the following types of food poisoning:

Infectious food poisoning
Toxic food poisoning

9. Explain **two** underlying principles of jam making.

(i)
(ii)

Leaving Certificate Examination 2024
Home Economics – Higher level
Section A and answerbook

10. Explain the following social welfare payments and give **one** example of each.

Social insurance payments
Social assistance payments

11. Identify **one** voluntary consumer protection agency.

Outline the role of the voluntary consumer protection agency named.

12. Outline the function of **each** of the following parts of a refrigerator:

the condenser
the evaporator

13. Outline **two** features of the current Irish National Housing Policy (Housing for All).

(i)
(ii)

14. Describe **two** different ways that consumers can be more environmentally conscious when choosing electrical goods.

(i)
(ii)

Answerbook for Sections B and C

Instructions

Questions for **Sections B** and **C** are supplied separately.

Start each question on a new page. Write the question number in the box at the top of each page. Use the left-hand column to label each part, as shown below.

You do not need to use all of the pages in this answerbook. If you run out of space in this answerbook, you may ask the superintendent for more paper.

Write your answers in blue or black pen. You may use pencil for sketches, graphs and diagrams only.

*New Format: From 2020 the returnable answerbook is provided with this section of the Exam Paper

Do not write on this page

Copyright notice
This examination paper may contain text or images for which the State Examinations Commission is not the copyright owner, and which may have been adapted, for the purpose of assessment, without the authors' prior consent. This examination paper has been prepared in accordance with Section 53(5) of the *Copyright and Related Rights Act, 2000*. Any subsequent use for a purpose other than the intended purpose is not authorised. The Commission does not accept liability for any infringement of third-party rights arising from unauthorised distribution or use of this examination paper.

Leaving Certificate – Higher Level

Home Economics - Scientific and Social Section A and Answerbook

Wednesday 5 June

Afternoon 2:00 - 4:30

2024.M48

2024L098A2EL

**Coimisiún na Scrúduithe Stáit
State Examinations Commission**

LEAVING CERTIFICATE EXAMINATION 2024

Home Economics – Scientific and Social

HIGHER LEVEL

Section B and Section C

WEDNESDAY 5 JUNE   AFTERNOON 2:00 – 4:30

Section B   180 marks
Answer **Question 1** and any other **two** questions from this section.
Question 1 is worth 80 marks.
Questions 2, 3, 4 and 5 are worth 50 marks each.

Section C   40 or 80 marks
Answer **one** elective question **or** Question 4 (core) to include **part (a)** and either **part (b) or (c)**.

If you submitted *Textiles, Fashion and Design* coursework for examination, you may only attempt Question 2 from this section.

Electives 1 and 3 are worth 80 marks each.
Elective 2 is worth 40 marks.
Question 4 (core) is worth 80 marks.

Do not hand this up.
This document will not be returned to the
State Examinations Commission.

Section B   180 marks

Answer **Question 1** and any other **two** questions from this section.
Question 1 is worth 80 marks. Questions 2, 3, 4 and 5 are worth 50 marks each.
Write your answer in the answerbook containing **Section A**.

Question 1

The Eurobarometer survey 2022 and 2019 questioned consumers on factors that affect their decisions when purchasing foods.

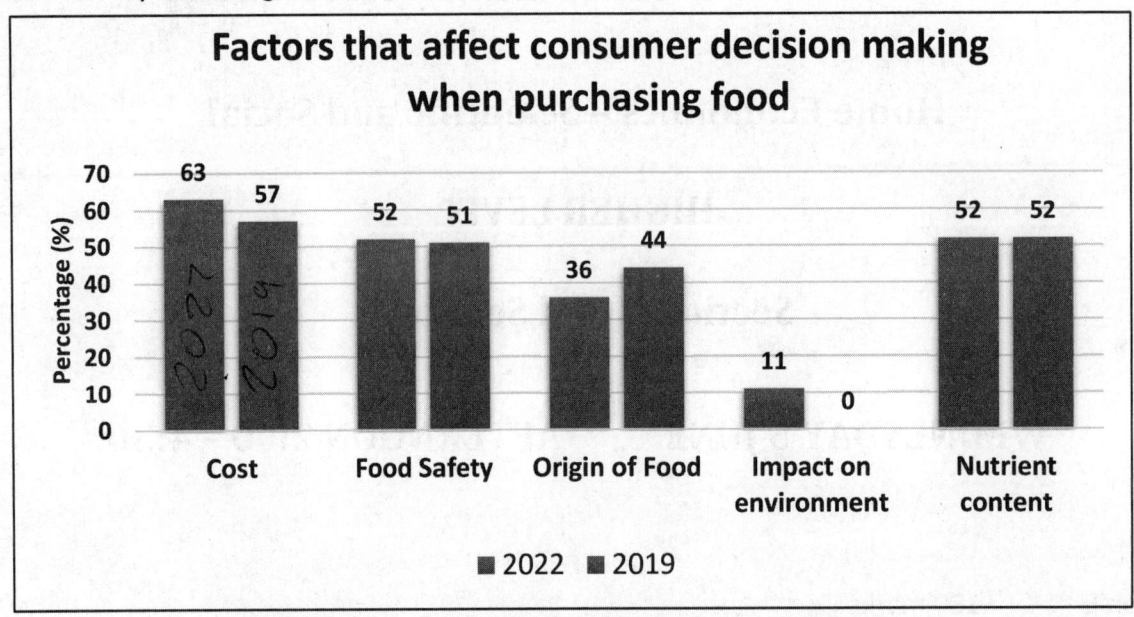

© European Food Safety Authority, 2019, 2022. *(adapted from www.efsa.europa.eu)*

(a) Using the information provided in the chart, comment and elaborate on **four** factors that affect consumer decisions when purchasing food.   (20 marks)

(b) Give a detailed account of carbohydrates and refer to:
- basic structure of a monosaccharide
- formation of disaccharides
- biological functions.   (22 marks)

(c) Describe **three** properties of sugar and give **one** culinary example of each property.
                                                                               (18 marks)

(d) Devise a set of strategies to follow when purchasing and preparing food/drink to reduce a person's sugar consumption.   (20 marks)

Leaving Certificate Examination 2024
Home Economics – Higher level
Sections B and C

Question 2
'A foetus is dependent on its mother for nutrition; so pregnant women must eat healthily and safely.'
(www.hse.ie)

(a) Discuss the dietary guidelines to follow when planning and preparing meals for a woman during pregnancy. (20 marks)

(b) Give an account of Folic Acid/Folate under **each** of the following headings:
- sources
- biological functions
- properties. (18 marks)

(c) Evaluate food labelling as a source of consumer information when purchasing foods for individuals with specific dietary requirements. (12 marks)

Question 3
'Artisan producers have altered Irish food culture to enrich our culinary heritage.'
(Irish Examiner Jan. 2023)

(a) Discuss the changes that have evolved in Irish food and eating patterns in recent years. (20 marks)

(b) Outline the stages involved in the manufacture of yogurt.
In your answer refer to production, packaging and labelling. (20 marks)

(c) Describe the protection provided to the consumer by the Food Hygiene Regulations 1950-1989. (10 marks)

Question 4

'Helpful, knowledgeable staff are the driving force behind in-store shopping being popular amongst Irish consumers.' *(www.pwc.ie)*

(a) Analyse the changes in consumer shopping patterns over the last decade. (20 marks)

(b) Name and evaluate **two** different methods of payment used by consumers to pay for in-store purchases. (18 marks)

(c) Describe the protection provided to the consumer by the Consumer Protection Act 2007. (12 marks)

Question 5

'The family is a dynamic, fluid, resilient and ever-changing fundamental institution of society.' *(Kristy Hawthorn)*

(a) Discuss the role of the family in meeting the physical and psychological needs of young children so that they will become well-adjusted adults in society. (20 marks)

(b) Analyse the impact of social, economic and technological changes on contemporary family structures. (18 marks)

(c) Describe **two** supports available to older family members and state how these supports help them to maintain their independence. (12 marks)

Section C   40 or 80 marks

Answer **one** elective question **or** Question 4 (core) to include **part (a)** and either **part (b)** or **(c)**.
If you submitted *Textiles, Fashion and Design* coursework for examination,
you may only attempt Question 2 from this section.
Write your answer in the answerbook containing **Section A**.

Elective 1 – Home Design and Management – 80 marks

Candidates selecting this elective must answer **1(a)** and either **1(b)** or **1(c)**.

1.(a) 'A well-planned, well-designed home looks elegant, and improves a person's quality of life.'
(www.homesandgardens.com)

   (i) Discuss the factors that influence the interior design of a home:
   Refer to:
   - cost
   - family size and circumstances
   - ergonomics.   (20 marks)

   (ii) Identify **three** design principles and describe how each design principle identified could be applied to an interior design space.   (18 marks)

   (iii) Evaluate how the design and construction of a house can help lower the energy use of its occupants.   (12 marks)

and

1.(b) 'Electricity is a powerful and versatile energy often taken for granted, but safe use is vital.'
(www.esbnetworks.com)

   (i) Describe how each of the following contribute to the safe use of electrical appliances in the home.
   - miniature circuit breaker
   - earth wire.   (12 marks)

   (ii) Identify **three** inefficient uses of energy in the home and assess a strategy you would recommend to improve the energy efficiency in each case identified.   (18 marks)

or

1.(c) 'If your home is well insulated; you also need good ventilation.'   *This content is reproduced courtesy of SEAI (www.seai.com)*

   (i) Explain the underlying principle of insulation used in the home.
   Identify and describe **three** different methods of home insulation.   (18 marks)

   (ii) Discuss the importance of having adequate ventilation in a house.   (12 marks)

Elective 2 – Textiles, Fashion and Design – 40 marks

Candidates selecting this elective must answer **2(a)** and either **2(b)** or **2(c)**.

2.(a) Being stylish, yet comfortable is key for many family gatherings and parties.

(*www.boohoo.com*) (*www.pinterest.com*)

(i) Evaluate the design of the outfits shown above for a summer family gathering.
Refer to:
- comfort
- aesthetic appeal
- current fashion trends. (15 marks)

(ii) Discuss how social and economic factors influence the design and construction of clothing. (10 marks)

and

2.(b) 'Natural fabrics are renewable; a good choice for sustainable living.' (*www.studioheijne.com*)

Write a profile of a fabric manufactured from natural fibres.
Refer to:
- fibre production
- fabric properties
- identification test. (15 marks)

or

2.(c) 'The fashion and textile industry continue to play its part in Ireland's social, cultural and economic development.' (*www.ndcg.ie*)

(i) Discuss the emergence of leisure wear as a current fashion trend. (6 marks)

(ii) Name **one** Irish fashion designer. Outline their work in the Irish fashion industry. (9 marks)

Elective 3 – Social Studies – 80 marks

Candidates selecting this elective must answer **3(a)** and either **3(b) or 3(c)**.

3.(a) 'Education gives people the opportunity and ability to improve their own lives.'
(www.legalstudymaterial.com)

    (i) Discuss the role of education in society.
Refer to education:
- as a method of socialisation
- as preparation for work. (20 marks)

    (ii) Evaluate a range of educational supports available in second level schools for students with special educational needs. (15 marks)

    (iii) Analyse how socio-economic status impacts equality of opportunity in education. (15 marks)

and

3.(b) While Ireland's unemployment figures are at a record low, some people may be excluded from the labour market.

    (i) Identify **three** groups of people who have difficulty in securing employment and discuss the reason why each group identified have high unemployment rates. (18 marks)

    (ii) Name and give details of **one** community-based initiative that helps to create employment. (12 marks)

or

3.(c) 'Leisure is not wasteful or an unproductive use of time; its benefits are far reaching.'
© Dr. Marcia Morris *(www.psychologytoday.com)*

    (i) Evaluate how individual and family leisure activities contribute to the physical, social and emotional development of family members. (18 marks)

    (ii) Analyse the social and cultural factors that influence an individual's choice of leisure activities. (12 marks)

Question 4 – Core – 80 marks

Candidates selecting this elective must answer **4(a)** and either **4(b)** or **4(c)**.

4.(a) 'Fats are essential for health; but choosing the correct types and amount is vital.'
(*www.fsai.ie*)

    (i) Evaluate the nutritional significance of fats and oils in the diet. (20 marks)

    (ii) Outline the stages involved in the production of margarine to include details of packaging and labelling. (15 marks)

    (iii) Assess the health implications for a person consuming a diet high in saturated fat. (15 marks)

and

4.(b) The use of household resources play a valuable role in everyday living.

    (i) Assess the selection criteria that should be considered when choosing household textiles. (12 marks)

    (ii) Set out details of a study you have carried out on **one** type of electrical appliance with a motor.
Refer to:
- working principle
- guidelines for use
- energy efficiency. (18 marks)

or

4.(c) 'Sensory analysis testing provides food developers and companies with valuable, insightful information.' (*www.intertek.com*)

    (i) Describe the conditions necessary to follow for sensory analysis testing in the classroom to ensure accurate results. (15 marks)

    (ii) Evaluate the role of artisan producers/small businesses in the Irish food industry. (15 marks)

**Do not hand this up.
This document will not be returned to the
State Examinations Commission.**

Copyright notice
This examination paper may contain text or images for which the State Examinations Commission is not the copyright owner, and which may have been adapted, for the purpose of assessment, without the authors' prior consent. This examination paper has been prepared in accordance with Section 53(5) of the *Copyright and Related Rights Act, 2000*. Any subsequent use for a purpose other than the intended purpose is not authorised. The Commission does not accept liability for any infringement of third-party rights arising from unauthorised distribution or use of this examination paper.

Leaving Certificate – Higher Level

Home Economics - Scientific and Social
Section B and Section C

Wednesday 5 June
Afternoon 2:00 – 4:30

6069.M48C

6069L098A1EC

Coimisiún na Scrúduithe Stáit
State Examinations Commission

Leaving Certificate Examination
Home Economics - Scientific and Social

Section A and Answerbook
Higher Level
2 hours 30 minutes
280 or 320 marks

Examination Number

Day and Month of Birth   For example, 3rd February is entered as 0302

Centre Stamp

Instructions

Write your Examination Number and your Day and Month of Birth in the boxes on the front cover.

Write your answers to all parts of the examination into this answerbook. This answerbook will be scanned and your work will be presented to an examiner on screen. Anything that you write outside of the answer areas may not be seen by the examiner.

Write your answers in blue or black pen. You may use pencil for sketches, graphs and diagrams only.

There are three sections to this examination. Questions for **Sections B and C** are supplied separately but your answers must be written in this answerbook.

Section A 60 marks
Answer any **ten** questions in this section.
Each question carries 6 marks.

Section B 180 marks
Answer **Question 1** and any other **two** questions from this section.
Question 1 is worth 80 marks.
Questions 2, 3, 4 and 5 are worth 50 marks each.

Section C 40 or 80 marks
Answer **one** elective question **or** Question 4 (core), to include **part (a)** and either **part (b) or part (c)**.

If you submitted *Textiles, Fashion and Design* coursework for examination, you may only attempt Question 2 from this section.

Electives 1 and 3 are worth 80 marks each.
Elective 2 is worth 40 marks.
Question 4 (core) is worth 80 marks.

Leaving Certificate – 2023 Deferred Paper
Home Economics – Higher Level

Section A   60 marks

Answer any **ten** questions from this section.
Each question carries 6 marks.
Write your answers in the spaces provided.

1. In relation to proteins, explain gel formation.

   Give **one** culinary example of gel formation.

2. Complete the table below in relation to the digestion of lipids.

Secretion	Enzyme	Substrate	Product
Pancreatic juice			

3. The following health conditions may result from a mineral deficiency in the diet.

   Identify **one** deficient mineral in each case.

Health Condition	Deficient Mineral
Rickets in children	
Muscular spasms and muscle cramps	
Enlargement of the thyroid gland	

Leaving Certificate – 2023 Deferred Paper
Home Economics – Higher Level

4. List **three** properties of Vitamin B1 (thiamine).

(i)
(ii)
(iii)

5. In relation to the diet, explain the term energy balance.

6. Name **three** different sectors in the Irish food industry and give **one** example of a food exported in each case.

Sector in the Irish food industry	Example of food exported

7. Outline **three** conditions that affect the growth of bacteria.

(i)
(ii)
(iii)

8. Explain the term 'added value food' and give **one** example of an added value food.

Added value food
Example

9. Outline **three** uses of sensory analysis in the food industry.

(i)
(ii)
(iii)

10. Describe **three** factors to consider when choosing a savings scheme.

(i)
(ii)
(iii)

11. Explain the following household insurance terms:

Policy
Premium

12. Identify **two** current features under Ireland's National Housing Policy.

(i)
(ii)

13. Outline **two** factors to consider when choosing household textiles.

(i)
(ii)

14. Name **one** cause of water pollution and state the effect of this pollution on the environment. Explain how water pollution can be reduced.

Cause
Effect
Reduction measure

Answerbook for Sections B and C

Instructions

Questions for **Sections B** and **C** are supplied separately.

Start each question on a new page. Write the question number in the box at the top of each page. Use the left-hand column to label each part, as shown below.

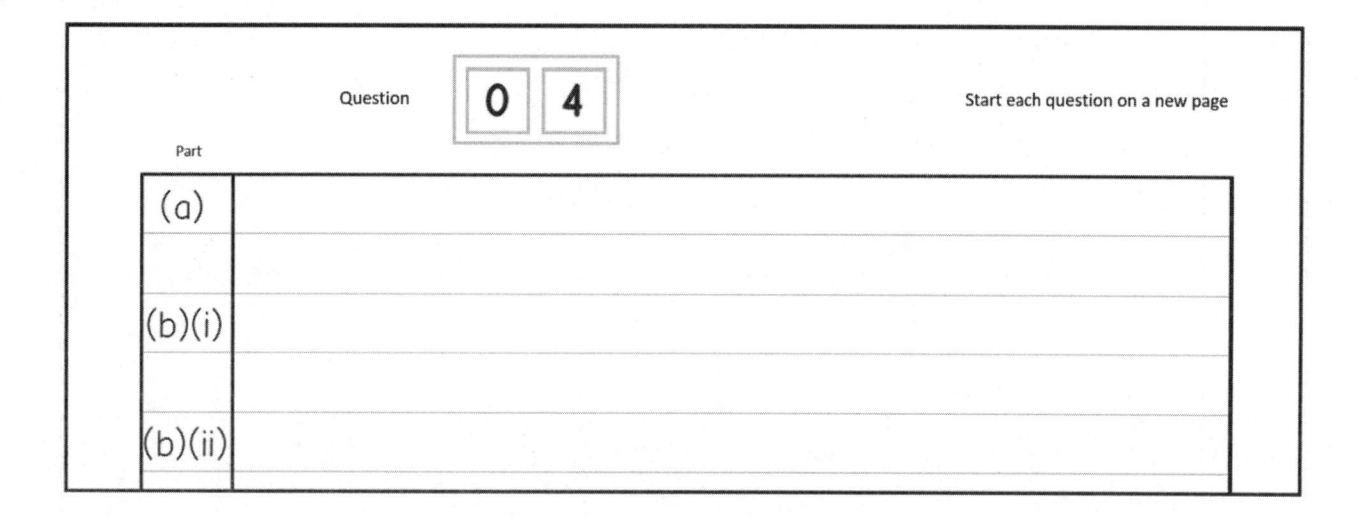

Part	Question **0 4** — Start each question on a new page
(a)	
(b)(i)	
(b)(ii)	

You do not need to use all of the pages in this answerbook. If you run out of space in this answerbook, you may ask the superintendent for more paper.

Write your answers in blue or black pen. You may use pencil for sketches, graphs and diagrams only.

*New Format: From 2020 the returnable answerbook is provided with this section of the Exam Paper

Leaving Certificate – 2023 Deferred Paper
Home Economics – Higher Level

Leaving Certificate – Higher Level

Home Economics - Scientific and Social
Section A and Answerbook

2 hours 30 minutes

6069.M48C

6069L098A2EC

Coimisiún na Scrúduithe Státit
State Examinations Commission

LEAVING CERTIFICATE EXAMINATION

Home Economics – Scientific and Social

HIGHER LEVEL

Section B and Section C

2 hours 30 minutes

Section B   180 marks
Answer **Question 1** and any other **two** questions from this section.
Question 1 is worth 80 marks.
Questions 2, 3, 4 and 5 are worth 50 marks each.

Section C   40 or 80 marks
Answer **one** elective question **or** Question 4 (core), to include **part (a)** and either **part (b) or part (c)**.

If you submitted *Textiles, Fashion and Design* coursework for examination, you may only attempt Question 2 from this section.

Electives 1 and 3 are worth 80 marks each.
Elective 2 is worth 40 marks.
Question 4 (core) is worth 80 marks.

Do not hand this up.
This document will not be returned to the
State Examinations Commission.

Section B
180 marks

Answer **Question 1** and any other **two** questions from this section.
Question 1 is worth 80 marks. Questions 2, 3, 4 and 5 are worth 50 marks each.
Write your answer in the answer book containing **Section A**.

Question 1
The following infographic shows the consumption of potatoes, pasta and rice as part of the evening meal among Irish adults aged 18 to 65+.

(*What Ireland Ate Last Night, Report 2020, Bord Bia Thinking House*)

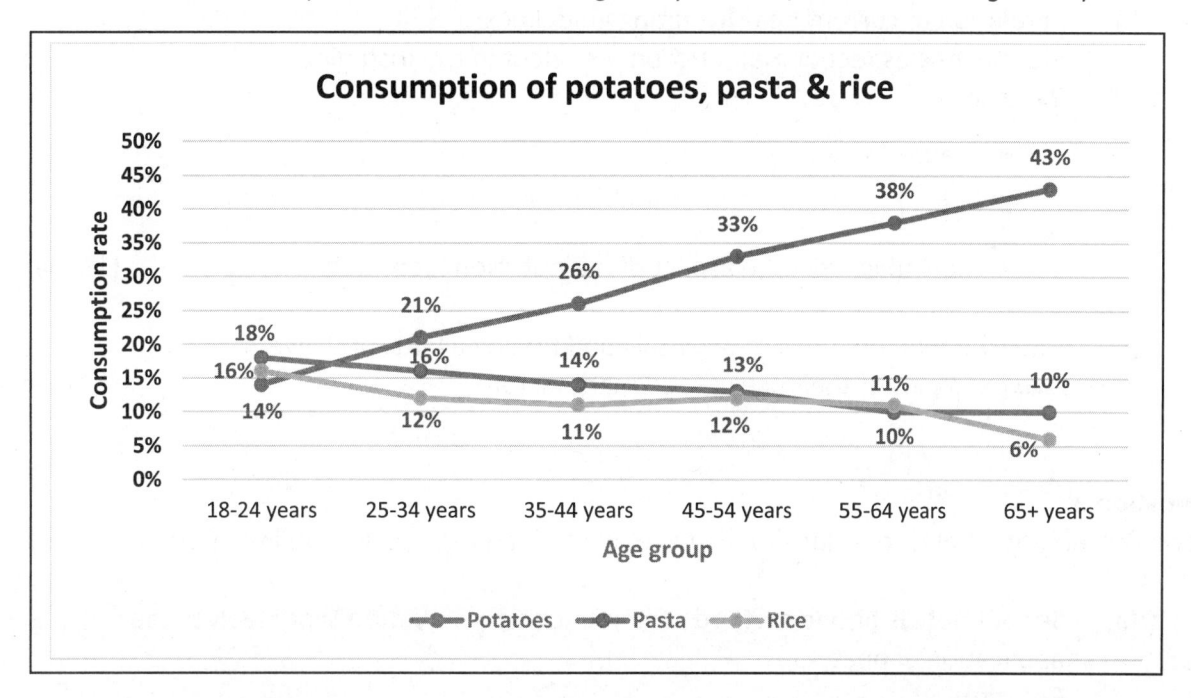

Consumption of potatoes, pasta & rice

Age group	Potatoes	Pasta	Rice
18-24 years	18%	14%	16%
25-34 years	16%	21%	12%
35-44 years	14%	26%	11%
45-54 years	13%	33%	12%
55-64 years	11%	38%	10%
65+ years	10%	43%	6%

(a) Using the information provided in the chart, comment and elaborate on the consumption of potatoes, pasta and rice among Irish adults. **(18 marks)**

(b) Classify carbohydrates and give **one** example of each class. **(12 marks)**

(c) Explain **each** of the following properties of carbohydrates:
- gelatinisation
- dextrinisation
- maillard reaction. **(18 marks)**

(d) Describe **three** factors that determine the energy requirements of an adult. **(12 marks)**

(e) Discuss the guidelines to follow when planning family meals and purchasing foods, to reduce the impact on the environment. **(20 marks)**

Leaving Certificate – 2023 Deferred Paper
Home Economics – Higher Level

Question 2

'Research reveals that up to one in every 100 people have coeliac disease and many more have an intolerance to gluten.' (*www.safefood.net*)

    (a)   Write an informative account of coeliac disease.
           Refer to:

- causes and symptoms
- specific dietary guidelines a coeliac should follow.   (22 marks)

    (b)   In relation to current healthy eating guidelines:
           Identify **one** aspect of malnutrition prevalent in the Irish diet.
           Refer to:

- cause
- effect
- how to correct the aspect of malnutrition identified.   (16 marks)

    (c)   Describe **two** functions of physical conditioning agents and give
           two examples of their use in food manufacture.   (12 marks)

Question 3

Food preservation helps to reduce food waste and to increase the availability of different foods.

    (a)   Set out details of **one** method of home food preservation that involves the application of heat.
           Refer to:

- name
- how the method of preservation is carried out
- the underlying principle.   (24 marks)

    (b)   Assess the use of **one** type of packaging material used in food processing.
           Refer to:

- name
- suitability of purpose
- environmental impact.   (18 marks)

    (c)   Outline the protection provided to the consumer by the Sale of Food and
           Drugs Acts (1875, 1879, 1899, 1936).   (8 marks)

Question 4

Kitchen appliances assist the consumer when cooking, cleaning, and storing food.

(a) Discuss **four** responsibilities a consumer has when purchasing kitchen appliances.

(16 marks)

(b) Set out details of a study you have carried out on a microwave oven.
Refer to:
- modern design features
- working principle
- guidelines for using the appliance.

(24 marks)

(c) Name and give details of **one** statutory agency that protects consumers. (10 marks)

Question 5

'62 per cent of people identified family and home as the biggest influences on their thinking.'

(*www.irishtimes.ie*)

(a) Explain the following sociological terms:
- culture
- norms
- role
- social mobility.

(20 marks)

(b) Analyse how economic and technological changes in recent times have affected the modern family.

(20 marks)

(c) Discuss the importance of good communication within the family. (10 marks)

Leaving Certificate – 2023 Deferred Paper
Home Economics – Higher Level

Section C 40 or 80 marks

Answer **one** elective question **or** Question 4 (core), to include **part (a)** and either **part (b) or (c)**.
If you submitted *Textiles, Fashion and Design* coursework for examination,
you may only attempt Question 2 from this section.
Write your answer in the answerbook containing **Section A**.

Elective 1 – Home Design and Management – 80 marks

Candidates selecting this elective must answer **1(a)** and either **1(b) or 1(c)**.

1.(a) 'It is estimated that Ireland will need an average of 33,000 new homes to be provided each year from 2021 to 2030.' (*www.gov.ie*)

(i) Outline the historical development of housing styles in Ireland from the nineteenth century to the present day. (20 marks)

(ii) Explain the housing requirements necessary to meet the needs of people who have a disability. (15 marks)

(iii) Evaluate the distribution of housing provision in Ireland today. (15 marks)

and

1.(b) 'Interior design is the art and science of enhancing the interior of a building.' (*wikipedia.org*)

(i) Describe how each of the following may impact the interior design of the home:
- aesthetic and comfort factors
- function of the room
- environmental awareness. (12 marks)

(ii) Explain **three** principles of interior design and give an example of the application of each principle in the home. (18 marks)

or

1.(c) 'There are lots of ways to make your home more energy efficient and comfortable.'
(*www.seai.ie*)

(i) In relation to household electricity supply describe each of the following:
- ring circuit
- miniature circuit breakers (MCBs)
- earth wire. (12 marks)

(ii) Identify **three** inefficient uses of electricity in the home and describe how to reduce the energy use in **each** case. (18 marks)

Leaving Certificate – 2023 Deferred Paper
Home Economics – Higher Level

Elective 2 – Textiles, Fashion and Design – 40 marks

Candidates selecting this elective must answer **2(a)** and either **2(b) or 2(c)**.

2.(a) A graduation ball allows young people the opportunity to dress formally for a celebratory occasion.

(*www.etiquettejulie.com*)

    (i)   Sketch and describe an outfit suitable to wear to a graduation ball.   (10 marks)

    (ii)   Evaluate the outfit with reference to each of the following:

- comfort
- aesthetic appeal
- suitability for purpose.   (15 marks)

and

2.(b) Natural fabric is clothing that is made from fibres produced by plants or animals.

Write a profile of one natural fabric you have studied.
Refer to:

- fibre production
- fabric properties
- fibre identification test.   (15 marks)

or

2.(c) The development of clothing trends is highly influenced by social and economic factors.

    (i)   Discuss how socio-economic factors influence the design and construction of clothing.   (9 marks)

    (ii)   Explain how social media influencers affect teenagers' choice of clothing.   (6 marks)

Elective 3 – Social Studies – 80 marks

Candidates selecting this elective must answer **3(a)** and either **3(b) or 3(c)**.

3.(a) 'Irish job attitudes survey says two-thirds of adults are happy in their jobs.' (*www.rte.ie*)

    (i) Differentiate between paid and unpaid work. (10 marks)

    (ii) Analyse the factors that have contributed to the increased participation rate of women in the Irish labour market. (20 marks)

    (iii) Identify and elaborate on the factors that affect an individual's attitude to work. (20 marks)

and

3.(b) There are many part-time and full-time education courses available to adults.

    (i) Analyse the factors that contribute to the increasing demand for adult and second chance education. (20 marks)

    (ii) Name and give details of **one** contemporary initiative that has improved access for adults to second chance education. (10 marks)

or

3.(c) 'Deciding on childcare is a big decision for any parent.' (*www.citizensinformation.ie*)

    (i) Analyse the key requirements that parents should consider when choosing a suitable childcare option. (20 marks)

    (ii) Evaluate **one** childcare option available to dual-earner families. (10 marks)

Leaving Certificate – 2023 Deferred Paper
Home Economics – Higher Level

Question 4 – Core – 80 marks

Candidates selecting this question must answer **4(a)** and either **4(b)** or **4(c)**.

4.(a) 'In Ireland, 8 in 10 consumers eat cheese in a typical week, with the majority consuming cheese 2-3 times a week.' (*www.bordbia.ie*)

    (i) Discuss the nutritional significance of cheese in the diet. (20 marks)

    (ii) Describe the production of cheese.
Refer to:
- stages of production
- packaging
- labelling. (20 marks)

    (iii) Give an account of the role of the Food Safety Authority of Ireland (FSAI). (10 marks)

and

4.(b) There are numerous shopping outlets available to Irish consumers.

    (i) Name **two** different types of retail outlets where household technology can be purchased.
State **one** advantage and **one** disadvantage of each outlet. (14 marks)

    (ii) Describe how the components of management (inputs, throughputs and outputs), could be applied to shopping efficiently for the family. (16 marks)

or

4.(c) Marriage is a big decision and is one of the most significant commitments in a person's life.

    (i) Describe **three** different cultural variations in marital arrangements. (15 marks)

    (ii) Discuss the rights and responsibilities of a couple within a marriage relationship. (15 marks)

Do not hand this up.
This document will not be returned to the
State Examinations Commission.

Copyright notice
This examination paper may contain text or images for which the State Examinations Commission is not the copyright owner, and which may have been adapted, for the purpose of assessment, without the authors' prior consent. This examination paper has been prepared in accordance with Section 53(5) *of the Copyright and Related Rights Act, 2000*. Any subsequent use for a purpose other than the intended purpose is not authorised. The Commission does not accept liability for any infringement of third-party rights arising from unauthorised distribution or use of this examination paper.

Leaving Certificate – Higher Level

Home Economics - Scientific and Social
Section B and Section C

2 hours 30 minutes

2023.M48

Coimisiún na Scrúduithe Stáit
State Examinations Commission

Leaving Certificate Examination 2023

Home Economics - Scientific and Social

Section A and Answerbook

Higher Level

Wednesday 7 June   Afternoon 2:00 - 4:30

280 or 320 marks

Examination Number

Day and Month of Birth

For example, 3rd February is entered as 0302

Centre Stamp

Instructions

Write your Examination Number and your Day and Month of Birth in the boxes on the front cover.

Write your answers to all parts of the examination into this answerbook. This answerbook will be scanned and your work will be presented to an examiner on screen. Anything that you write outside of the answer areas may not be seen by the examiner.

Write your answers in blue or black pen. You may use pencil for sketches, graphs and diagrams only.

There are three sections in this examination. Questions for **Sections B and C** are supplied separately but your answers must be written in this answerbook.

Section A 60 marks
Answer any **ten** questions in this section.
Each question carries 6 marks.

Section B 180 marks
Answer **Question 1** and any other **two** questions from this section.
Question 1 is worth 80 marks.
Questions 2, 3, 4 and 5 are worth 50 marks each.

Section C 40 or 80 marks
Answer **one** elective question **or** Question 4 (core) to include **part (a)** and either **part (b) or (c)**.

If you submitted *Textiles, Fashion and Design* coursework for examination, you may only attempt Question 2 from this section.

Electives 1 and 3 are worth 80 marks each.
Elective 2 is worth 40 marks.
Question 4 (core) is worth 80 marks.

Section A

60 marks

Answer any **ten** questions from this section.
Each question carries 6 marks.
Write your answers in the spaces provided.

1. State **two** biological functions of lipids.

   (i)

   (ii)

2. Explain the term gelatinisation and include **one** culinary example in your answer.

3. Name **two** food poisoning bacteria and give an example of a different high-risk food associated with each.

Name of food poisoning bacteria	high-risk food

4. Explain the term Basal Metabolic Rate (BMR).

Give **two** factors that affect a person's basal metabolic rate.

(i)

(ii)

5. Describe a roux-based sauce and give **one** culinary example.

6. Outline **two** benefits of including high fibre foods in the diet of adults.

(i)

(ii)

7. Describe **two** chemical changes that occur when food is cooked.

(i)
(ii)

8. Name **one** sensory analysis test used to determine a preferred product from two or more samples.

Describe **two** different uses of sensory analysis in the food industry.

(i)
(ii)

9. Outline the role of public analyst laboratories in relation to food safety.

10. Describe the Working Family Payment (WFP) (formerly Family Income Supplement) as a social welfare payment.

11. Outline **two** measures consumers can implement in their daily lives to prevent/reduce air pollution.

Measures to prevent/reduce air pollution
(i)
(ii)

12. Explain the following types of mortgage interest rates.

Fixed rate
Variable rate

13. Describe the importance of each of the following when selecting a savings scheme.

Interest payable
Access to funds

14. Explain how the Consumer Credit Act, 1995 benefits the consumer.

(i)
(ii)

Answerbook for Sections B and C

Instructions

Questions for **Sections B** and **C** are supplied separately.

Start each question on a new page. Write the question number in the box at the top of each page. Use the left-hand column to label each part, as shown below.

	Question 0 4	Start each question on a new page
Part		
(a)		
(b)(i)		
(b)(ii)		

You do not need to use all of the pages in this answerbook. If you run out of space in this answerbook, you may ask the superintendent for more paper.

Write your answers in blue or black pen. You may use pencil for sketches, graphs and diagrams only.

*****New Format**: From 2020 the returnable answerbook is provided with this section of the Exam Paper

Do not write on this page

Copyright notice
This examination paper may contain text or images for which the State Examinations Commission is not the copyright owner, and which may have been adapted, for the purpose of assessment, without the authors' prior consent. This examination paper has been prepared in accordance with *Section 53(5) of the Copyright and Related Rights Act, 2000*. Any subsequent use for a purpose other than the intended purpose is not authorised. The Commission does not accept liability for any infringement of third-party rights arising from unauthorised distribution or use of this examination paper.

Leaving Certificate – Higher Level

Home Economics - Scientific and Social Section A and Answerbook

Wednesday 7 June

Afternoon 2:00 - 4:30

2023.M48

2023L098A2EL

Coimisiún na Scrúduithe Stáit
State Examinations Commission

LEAVING CERTIFICATE EXAMINATION 2023

Home Economics – Scientific and Social

HIGHER LEVEL

Section B and Section C

WEDNESDAY 7 JUNE   AFTERNOON 2:00 – 4:30

Section B
180 marks
Answer **Question 1** and any other **two** questions from this section.
Question 1 is worth 80 marks.
Questions 2, 3, 4 and 5 are worth 50 marks each.

Section C
40 or 80 marks
Answer **one** elective question **or** Question 4 (core) to include **part (a)** and either **part (b) or (c)**.

If you submitted *Textiles, Fashion and Design* coursework for examination, you may only attempt Question 2 from this section.

Electives 1 and 3 are worth 80 marks each.
Elective 2 is worth 40 marks.
Question 4 (core) is worth 80 marks.

Do not hand this up.
This document will not be returned to the
State Examinations Commission.

Section B | **180 marks**

Answer **Question 1** and any other **two** questions from this section.
Question 1 is worth 80 marks. Questions 2, 3, 4 and 5 are worth 50 marks each.
Write your answer in the answerbook containing **Section A**.

Question 1
'Adequate micronutrient intake during the teenage years is important for optimum growth and development.' *(National Teen Food Survey II Report 2021 adapted from iuna.net)*

Sources of Iron in Irish teenagers aged 13-18 years

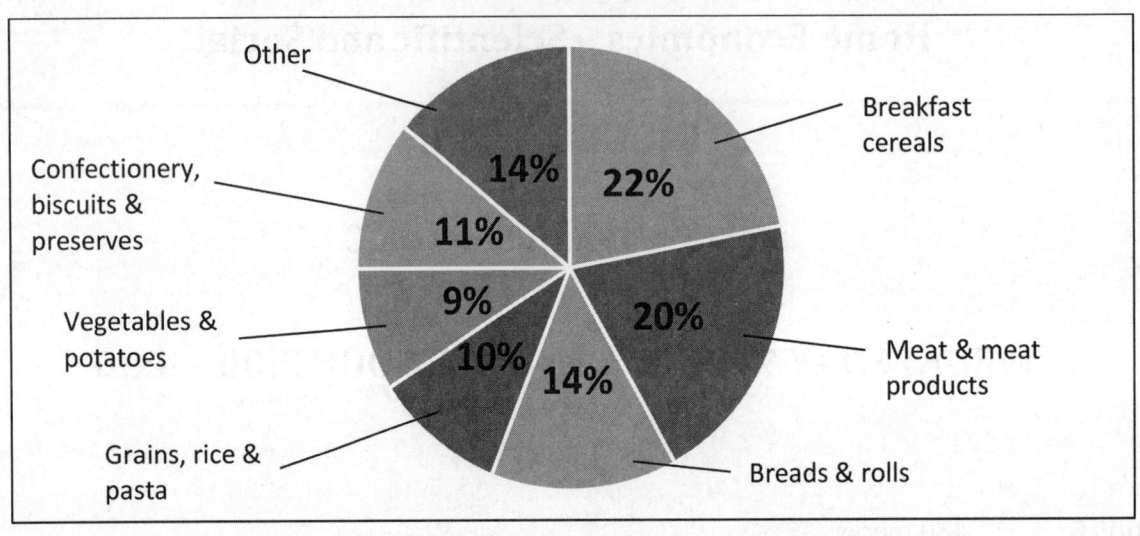

- Other: 14%
- Breakfast cereals: 22%
- Confectionery, biscuits & preserves: 11%
- Vegetables & potatoes: 9%
- Meat & meat products: 20%
- Grains, rice & pasta: 10%
- Breads & rolls: 14%

(a) Using the information provided in the chart, comment and elaborate on the importance of including different sources of iron in a teenagers' diet.
Refer to **four** sources in your answer. (20 marks)

(b) Identify and describe the factors that affect the absorption of iron in the body. (20 marks)

(c) Give an account of Vitamin C with reference to:
- biological functions
- effects of deficiency
- properties. (20 marks)

(d) Discuss the guidelines a family should follow, when doing their weekly shopping on a restricted budget, in order to provide for their nutritional needs. (20 marks)

Question 2
'Nutritional experts recommend consuming 2-3 portions of fish each week for a balanced diet.'
(www.goodfoodireland.ie)

    (a)   Discuss the nutritional significance of fish in the diet.   (20 marks)

    (b)   Give a detailed account of **one** process used to extend the shelf life of fish.
           Refer to:
- name
- underlying principle
- effects.   (18 marks)

    (c)   Describe the role of the Food Safety Authority of Ireland (FSAI) in the food industry.   (12 marks)

Question 3
'People are becoming more experimental in their culinary choices.' (www.bordbia.ie)

    (a)   Discuss the factors that affect food choices for families today.   (12 marks)

    (b)   Profile an added value food you have studied.
           Refer to:
- name
- stages of production
- packaging and labelling.   (26 marks)

    (c)   Name and describe the role of **one** physical conditioning agent used in food processing.   (12 marks)

2023 HL

Question 4

'Consumers must be constantly vigilant to protect themselves.' (*www.thecai.ie*)

    (a)   Discuss how the following factors affect the management of the home.

- stages in the life cycle of the family
- employment patterns
- values.   (20 marks)

    (b)   Analyse how different techniques used by retailers influence consumer spending.

(20 marks)

    (c)   Describe how the responsibilities of a consumer can assist them in making wise choices.   (10 marks)

Question 5

The family is an integral social institution in society.

    (a)   Discuss the changes that have taken place in the family from the middle of the twentieth century to the present day.   (20 marks)

    (b)   Explain the following sociological terms:

- universality of the family
- kinship
- monogamy.   (15 marks)

    (c)   Describe **one** legal option available in Ireland to couples when their marriage has broken down.   (15 marks)

Section C
40 or 80 marks

Answer **one** elective question **or** Question 4 (core) to include **part (a)** and either **part (b) or (c)**.
If you submitted *Textiles, Fashion and Design* coursework for examination,
you may only attempt Question 2 from this section.
Write your answer in the answerbook containing **Section A**.

Elective 1 – Home Design and Management – 80 marks

Candidates selecting this elective must answer **1(a)** and either **1(b) or 1(c)**.

1.(a) 'Ireland's *Better Energy Warmer Homes* scheme aims to help people make their home warmer, healthier and cheaper to run.' (*www.seai.ie*)

  (i) Describe the factors that influence interior design in the home.
  Refer to:
  - aesthetic and comfort factors
  - environmental awareness. (20 marks)

  (ii) Discuss levels of thermal comfort in relation to **two** different living spaces in the home. (12 marks)

  (iii) Explain the underlying principle of a thermostat and describe how it can be used in the home. (18 marks)

and

1.(b) 'Lighting ideas are an essential part of space design.' (*www.homesandgardens.com*)

  (i) Describe **four** properties of light and give an example of how each property is used in the home. (20 marks)

  (ii) Explain the underlying principle of **one** type of energy-efficient lighting. (10 marks)

or

1.(c) 'We have been forced to rethink how we live in our homes in recent years.' (*The Irish Times*)

  (i) Discuss how environmental, economic and social factors influence the choice of housing styles in Ireland today. (18 marks)

  (ii) Describe the impact of burning fossil fuels in the home.
  Refer to:
  - an emission produced by burning fossil fuels
  - effects on the environment
  - a strategy households could implement in order to reduce emissions.

  (12 marks)

Elective 2 – Textiles, Fashion and Design – 40 marks

Candidates selecting this elective must answer **2(a)** and either **2(b)** or **2(c)**.

2.(a) A special occasion is an opportunity for an individual to showcase their unique sense of style.

    (i) Sketch and describe an outfit to wear for your graduation ball. (12 marks)

    (ii) Suggest a suitable fabric for the outfit and give a reason for your choice. (6 marks)

    (iii) Name **one** design principle and evaluate how it applies to your outfit. (7 marks)

and

2.(b) Blended fabrics have combined properties of each component fibre.

Write a profile of **one** blended fabric.
Refer to:
- fabric production
- fabric properties
- uses. (15 marks)

or

2.(c) 'The vintage clothing industry is growing 25 times faster than the overall retail market.'
(www.rediscoverycentre.ie)

    (i) Discuss the emergence of vintage clothing as a current fashion trend.
Refer to:
- pattern
- influences
- accessories. (9 marks)

    (ii) Name and give details of **one** career opportunity in the clothing and textile industry. (6 marks)

Elective 3 – Social Studies – 80 marks

Candidates selecting this elective must answer **3(a)** and either **3(b) or 3(c)**.

3.(a) 'We are currently witnessing the nature of employment being redefined in Ireland and across the world.' (*www.skillnetireland.ie*)

- **(i)** Discuss how technology and increasing flexibility in working hours affect patterns of work and work availability. (20 marks)

- **(ii)** Describe the impact of dual-earner families on family life.
  Refer to:
    - role overload
    - role conflict
    - distribution of parental responsibilities in the home. (15 marks)

- **(iii)** Recommend **one** type of child care option available to working parents.
  Analyse how the chosen child care option meets the requirements of the family. (15 marks)

and

3.(b) 'One in every nine people in Ireland lives on an income below the poverty line.'
(*poverty focus 2022, socialjusticeireland.ie*)

- **(i)** Analyse the following as contributory factors to poverty in Ireland today.
    - cycle of deprivation in geographical areas
    - the influence of social policy on poverty. (16 marks)

- **(ii)** Name and give details of **two** statutory schemes that reduce expenditure for low-income families. (14 marks)

or

3.(c) 'Contemporary society is experiencing rapid social change.' (*Social Change Research Group, wit.ie*)

- **(i)** Analyse the impact of social change on the family.
  Refer to:
    - changing attitudes to marriage
    - parenting roles
    - increased participation of women in the workforce. (18 marks)

- **(ii)** Describe how the Protection of Young Persons (Employment), Act 1996 offers protection to young people in work. (12 marks)

Question 4 – Core – 80 marks

Candidates selecting this elective must answer **4(a)** and either **4(b) or 4(c)**.

4.(a) 'The meat sector in Ireland is one of the most important industries in the national economy.'
(www.ibec.ie)

   (i) Discuss the measures that have been implemented in the Irish food industry to ensure meat is safe for consumption. **(12 marks)**

   (ii) Meat is a versatile food and can be cooked in a variety of ways.
Evaluate **one** method of cooking meat.
Refer to:
- name of cooking method
- underlying principle
- how the cooking method chosen affects the meat. **(24 marks)**

   (iii) Identify a type of material suitable for packaging perishable foods.
Assess the suitability for purpose and environmental impact of the material identified. **(14 marks)**

and

4.(b) Everyday living includes many transactions that require consumer spending.

   (i) Evaluate the socio-economic factors that impact household expenditure. **(15 marks)**

   (ii) Describe how the state assists the family in carrying out its economic function in society. **(15 marks)**

or

4.(c) 'Irish people are cooking more at home, and how we shop for food, cook and eat has changed significantly.' *(The Irish Times)*

   (i) Evaluate the contribution of the microwave oven to the management of the home. **(15 marks)**

   (ii) Describe the working principle of the microwave oven. **(15 marks)**

**Do not hand this up.
This document will not be returned to the
State Examinations Commission.**

Copyright notice
This examination paper may contain text or images for which the State Examinations Commission is not the copyright owner, and which may have been adapted, for the purpose of assessment, without the authors' prior consent. This examination paper has been prepared in accordance with Section 53(5) of the *Copyright and Related Rights Act, 2000*. Any subsequent use for a purpose other than the intended purpose is not authorised. The Commission does not accept liability for any infringement of third-party rights arising from unauthorised distribution or use of this examination paper.

Leaving Certificate – Higher Level

Home Economics - Scientific and Social
Section B and Section C

Wednesday 7 June
Afternoon 2:00 – 4:30

2022.M48C

2022L098A1EC

Coimisiún na Scrúduithe Stáit
State Examinations Commission

Leaving Certificate Examination

Home Economics – Scientific and Social

Section A and Answerbook

Higher Level

2 hours 30 minutes

200 or 240 marks

Examination Number

Day and Month of Birth

For example, 3rd February is entered as 0302

Centre Stamp

Instructions

Write your Examination Number and your Day and Month of Birth in the boxes on the front cover.

Write your answers to all parts of the examination into this answerbook. This answerbook will be scanned and your work will be presented to an examiner on screen. Anything that you write outside of the answer areas may not be seen by the examiner.

Write your answers in blue or black pen. You may use pencil for sketches, graphs and diagrams only.

There are three sections to this examination. Questions for **Sections B and C** are supplied separately but your answers must be written in this answerbook.

Section A   30 marks
Answer any **five** questions in this section.
Each question carries 6 marks.

Section B   130 marks
Answer **Question 1** and **one** question from questions 2, 3, 4 and 5.
Question 1 is worth 80 marks.
Questions 2, 3, 4 and 5 are worth 50 marks each.

Section C   40 or 80 marks
Answer **one** elective question **or** Question 4 (core) to include **part (a)** and either **part (b) or (c)**.

If you submitted *Textiles, Fashion and Design* coursework for examination, you may only attempt Question 2 from this section.

Electives 1 and 3 are worth 80 marks each.
Elective 2 is worth 40 marks.
Question 4 (core) is worth 80 marks.

Leaving Certificate – 2022 Deferred Paper
Home Economics – Higher Level

Section A   30 marks

Answer any **five** questions from this section.
Each question carries 6 marks.
Write your answers in the spaces provided.

1. State **two** properties of protein.

(i)
(ii)

   What is mycoprotein?

2. In relation to carbohydrates, explain each of the following terms:

Maillard reaction
Carmelisation

3. Explain Basal Metabolic Rate (BMR).

   List **two** factors that affect energy requirements.

(i)
(ii)

Leaving Certificate – 2022 Deferred Paper
Home Economics – Higher Level

4. The conditions listed below are caused by a deficiency in the diet of specific vitamins. Identify the vitamin in each case.

Anaemia	
Rickets	
Beriberi	

5. Explain each of the following:

Haem iron
Non-haem iron

6. Define diabetes.

State **two** factors which should be considered when planning meals for a person who is a diabetic.

(i)
(ii)

7. Complete the following table in relation to soup:

Classification	Example
Thick soups	
Thin/Clear soups	
Cold soups	

8. What is irradiated food?

State **two** effects of irradiation on food.

(i)	
(ii)	

9. In relation to food safety, explain each of the following:

Food contaminants
Cross contamination

Leaving Certificate – 2022 Deferred Paper
Home Economics – Higher Level

10. State the purpose of family resource management systems.

List **three** components of family resource management systems.

11. State the function of the following parts of the refrigerator:

Condenser
Thermostat

12. Name a fire/flame retardant finish used on household furnishings.

Outline **two** effects of this finish.

(i)
(ii)

Leaving Certificate – 2022 Deferred Paper
Home Economics – Higher Level

13. Identify **two** conditions necessary to qualify for the Working Family Payment (Family Income Supplement).

(i)
(ii)

14. Outline **two** functions of the Money Advice and Budgeting Service (MABS).

(i)
(ii)

Answerbook for Sections B and C

Instructions

Questions for **Sections B** and **C** are supplied separately.

Start each question on a new page. Write the question number in the box at the top of each page. Use the left-hand column to label each part, as shown below.

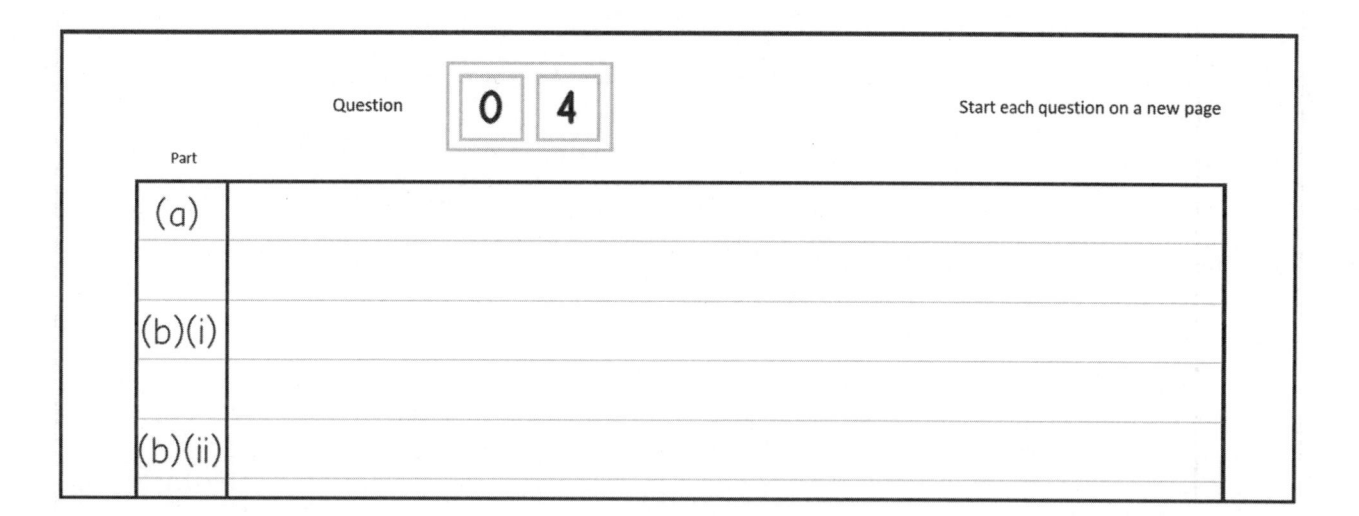

Part	Question 0 4 — Start each question on a new page
(a)	
(b)(i)	
(b)(ii)	

You do not need to use all of the pages in this answerbook. If you run out of space in this answerbook, you may ask the superintendent for more paper.

Write your answers in blue or black pen. You may use pencil for sketches, graphs and diagrams only.

***New Format**: From 2020 the returnable answerbook is provided with this section of the Exam Paper

Leaving Certificate – 2022 Deferred Paper
Home Economics – Higher Level

Do not write on this page

Copyright notice
This examination paper may contain text or images for which the State Examinations Commission is not the copyright owner, and which may have been adapted, for the purpose of assessment, without the authors' prior consent. This examination paper has been prepared in accordance with *Section 53(5) of the Copyright and Related Rights Act, 2000*. Any subsequent use for a purpose other than the intended purpose is not authorised. The Commission does not accept liability for any infringement of third-party rights arising from unauthorised distribution or use of this examination paper.

Leaving Certificate – Higher Level

Home Economics – Scientific and Social Section A and Answerbook

2 hours 30 minutes

2022. M48C

2022L098A2EC

Coimisiún na Scrúduithe Stáit
State Examinations Commission

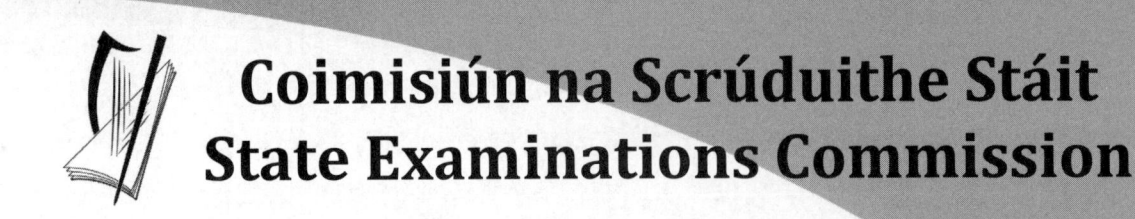

LEAVING CERTIFICATE EXAMINATION

Home Economics – Scientific and Social

HIGHER LEVEL

Section B and Section C

2 hours 30 minutes

Section B 130 marks
Answer **Question 1** and **one** question from questions 2, 3, 4 and 5.
Question 1 is worth 80 marks.
Questions 2, 3, 4 and 5 are worth 50 marks each.

Section C 40 or 80 marks
Answer **one** elective question **or** Question 4 (core) to include **part (a)** and either **part (b) or (c)**.

If you submitted *Textiles, Fashion and Design* coursework for examination, you may only attempt Question 2 from this section.

Electives 1 and 3 are worth 80 marks each.
Elective 2 is worth 40 marks.
Question 4 (core) is worth 80 marks.

Do not hand this up.
This document will not be returned to the State Examinations Commission.

Section B   130 marks

Answer **Question 1** and **one** question from questions 2, 3, 4 and 5.
Question 1 is worth 80 marks. Questions 2, 3, 4 and 5 are worth 50 marks each.
Write your answer in the answerbook containing **Section A**.

Question 1
The chart below presents information on the reasons why consumers consult food labels.

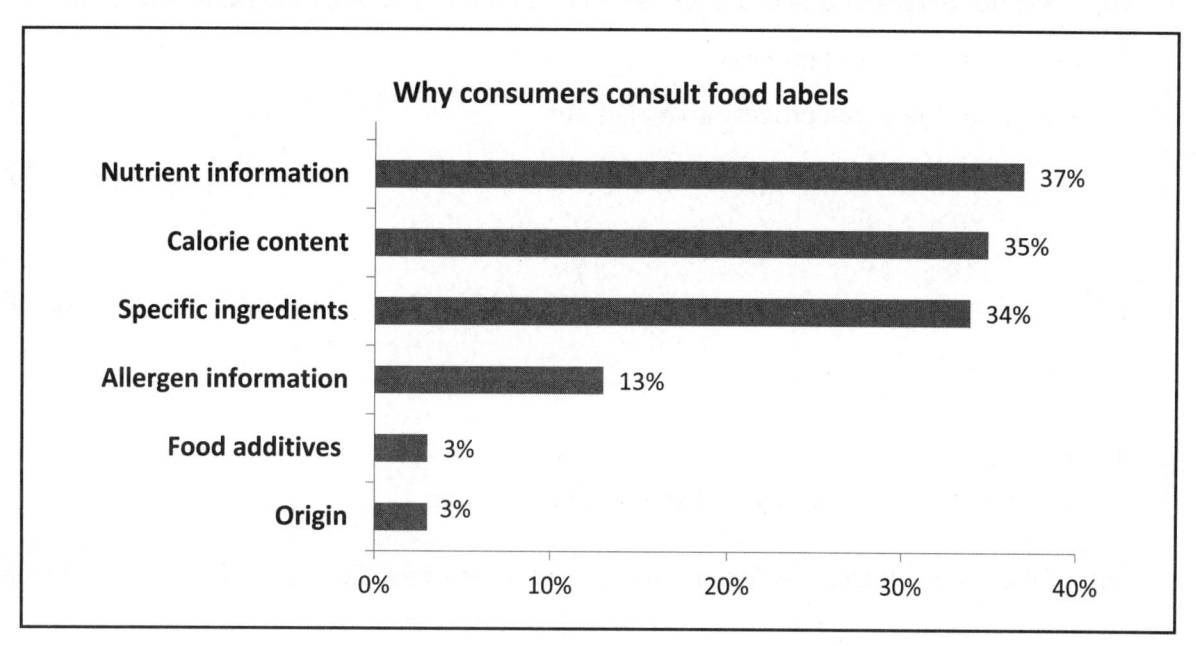

Why consumers consult food labels

- Nutrient information: 37%
- Calorie content: 35%
- Specific ingredients: 34%
- Allergen information: 13%
- Food additives: 3%
- Origin: 3%

(*adapted from a Research Study into Consumers' Attitudes to Food Labelling - FSAI*)

(a) Using the information provided in the table above, comment and elaborate on **four** reasons why consumers read food labels. *(20 marks)*

(b) Give an account of lipids (fats) and refer to:
- structure
- biological functions. *(28 marks)*

(c) Explain each of the following terms associated with fats and oils:
- rancidity
- smoke point. *(12 marks)*

(d) Identify and discuss how a person's health status might influence decision making when purchasing food products. *(20 marks)*

Question 2

Irish agri-food and drink exports amounted to approximately €13 billion in 2019, with the beef sector accounting for €2.25 billion. (www.bordbia.ie)

(a) Discuss **four** factors that contribute to the continued success of the food and drinks industry in Ireland. (16 marks)

(b) Set out details of **one** process used to extend the shelf life of meat and refer to:
- name of process
- how the process is carried out
- the underlying principle involved. (22 marks)

(c) Outline the role of **one** national agency in relation to food safety. (12 marks)

Question 3

When it comes to healthy food, eggs are the real superheroes.

(a) Discuss the nutritive value and the contribution of eggs to the diet. (20 marks)

(b) Name and explain the properties of eggs and their related culinary uses. (18 marks)

(c) Explain how quality is assured in egg production in order to minimise food safety risks. (12 marks)

Leaving Certificate – 2022 Deferred Paper
Home Economics – Higher Level

Question 4

Consumers require good quality information when choosing and buying goods and services.

(a) Identify the changes in consumer shopping patterns in recent years and discuss the reasons for the changes you have identified. (20 marks)

(b) Discuss **four** in-store techniques that supermarkets use to encourage consumer spending. (20 marks)

(c) Name and outline the role of **one** voluntary agency concerned with consumer protection. (10 marks)

Question 5

Family structures are diverse in modern Irish society.

(a) Analyse the changes in family structures in today's society. (18 marks)

(b) Discuss the social, economic and technological changes that affect families in Ireland. (20 marks)

(c) Outline the protection provided to families by The Family Law (Maintenance of Spouses and Children) Act 1976. (12 marks)

Section C **40 or 80 marks**

Answer **one** elective question **or** Question 4 (core) to include part **(a)** and either **part (b)** or **(c)**.
If you submitted *Textiles, Fashion and Design* coursework for examination,
you may only attempt Question 2 from this section.
Write your answer in the answerbook containing **Section A**.

Elective 1 – Home Design and Management – 80 marks

Candidates selecting this elective must answer **1(a)** and either **1(b)** or **1(c)**.

1.(a) The table below shows a comparison of energy costs and efficiency ratings for a variety of fuel used to heat a room in 2020.   (*www.seai.ie*)

Fuel	Energy Cost – cent/kWh	Efficiency rating
Standard coal	5.66	60%
Kerosene (oil)	8.60	80%
Natural gas (Band D2)	6.86	90%
Electricity (Band DE)	17.77	100%
Electricity - night rate	9.60	

(i) Using the information in the table, comment on the merits of heating a room using the fuels listed. (16 marks)

(ii) Describe **one** type of central heating system suitable for a family home.
Refer to:
- type of heating system
- underlying principle
- reasons for choice. (24 marks)

(iii) Recommend **one** method of insulation suitable for the walls of a house. Explain the underlying principle involved in your choice of insulation. (10 marks)

and

1.(b) The design of new homes has changed the Irish landscape.

(i) Describe **three** recent changes in the design of housing in Ireland. (18 marks)

(ii) Name and give details of **one** grant provision/scheme available to home owners. (12 marks)

or

1.(c) Householders who are more energy aware can reduce energy use by up to 20%.

(i) In relation to energy use in the home, identify potential energy inefficiencies and strategies for their improvement. (18 marks)

(ii) Identify the emissions produced as a result of burning fuels in the home and describe the effects of these emissions on the environment. (12 marks)

Leaving Certificate – 2022 Deferred Paper
Home Economics – Higher Level

Elective 2 – Textiles, Fashion and Design – 40 marks

Candidates selecting this elective must answer **2(a)** and either **2(b) or 2(c)**.

2.(a) Smart casual clothing is a requirement for many men and women in the workplace.

    (i)   Sketch and describe a smart casual outfit suitable for work wear.   (10 marks)

    (ii)   In relation to the outfit give details of:
- how **three** principles of design have been applied
- how the outfit is suitable for purpose.   (15 marks)

and

2.(b) The use of blended fabrics in clothing can have many benefits.

Write a profile of **one** fabric manufactured from blended fibres.
Refer to:
- name
- fibre production
- fabric properties
- uses.   (15 marks)

or

2.(c) (i) Describe the different sectors that comprise the Irish clothing market.   (6 marks)

    (ii)   Discuss how technology has influenced the design and construction of modern clothing.   (9 marks)

Leaving Certificate – 2022 Deferred Paper
Home Economics – Higher Level

Elective 3 – Social Studies – 80 marks

Candidates selecting this elective must answer **3(a)** and either **3(b) or 3(c)**.

3.(a) Education is now widely recognised and accepted as a critical driver of economic success and social progress in modern society.

    (i)   Discuss the purpose of education in relation to the physical, emotional, moral and intellectual development of the individual. (24 marks)

    (ii)   Comment on how socio-economic status impacts on equality of opportunity in education. (16 marks)

    (iii)   Name and give details of **one** contemporary initiative that improves access to education. (10 marks)

and

3.(b) Poverty remains an immense challenge in today's society.

    (i)   Identify **two** groups at risk of experiencing poverty in Ireland and discuss the impact of poverty on the family and society. (18 marks)

    (ii)   Analyse how each of the following has impacted on the current rates of poverty:
- the cycle of poverty
- social policy on poverty. (12 marks)

or

3.(c) The number of dual-earner families has increased significantly in recent years.

    (i)   Analyse the impact of dual-earner families on family life. (12 marks)

    (ii)   Name and evaluate **two** types of childcare options that are available to parents. (18 marks)

Leaving Certificate – 2022 Deferred Paper
Home Economics – Higher Level

Question 4 – Core – 80 marks
Candidates selecting this question must answer **4(a)** and either **4(b) or 4(c)**.

4.(a) 'Milk is a natural, delicious and nutritious drink'. (*National Dairy Council*)

    (i) Discuss the nutritional significance of milk in the diet. (20 marks)

    (ii) In relation to osteoporosis discuss:

- the main factors that increase the risk of developing osteoporosis
- the effects of osteoporosis on the body. (18 marks)

    (iii) Outline the reasons why dairy products are a major Irish export. (12 marks)

and

4.(b) Some bacteria are harmful, but most serve a useful purpose.

    (i) Discuss **four** conditions necessary for the growth of bacteria. (20 marks)

    (ii) Outline **two** uses of micro-organisms in food production. (10 marks)

or

4.(c) 'Ireland is going to have to rebuild its economy, for the second time in a decade'.
(*The Irish Times, 2020*)

    (i) Outline the role of the family as a financial unit within the economy. (12 marks)

    (ii) Identify and explain **four** factors that may contribute to varying patterns of household expenditure. (18 marks)

Leaving Certificate – 2022 Deferred Paper
Home Economics – Higher Level

Do not hand this up.
This document will not be returned to the State Examinations Commission.

Copyright notice
This examination paper may contain text or images for which the State Examinations Commission is not the copyright owner, and which may have been adapted, for the purpose of assessment, without the authors' prior consent. This examination paper has been prepared in accordance with Section 53(5) of the Copyright and Related Rights Act, 2000. Any subsequent use for a purpose other than the intended purpose is not authorised. The Commission does not accept liability for any infringement of third-party rights arising from unauthorised distribution or use of this examination paper.

Leaving Certificate – Higher Level

Home Economics - Scientific and Social
Section B and Section C

2 hours 30 minutes

2022.M48

Coimisiún na Scrúduithe Stáit
State Examinations Commission

Leaving Certificate Examination 2022

Home Economics – Scientific and Social

Section A and Answerbook

Higher Level

Wednesday 8 June   Afternoon 2:00 - 4:30

200 or 240 marks

Examination Number

Day and Month of Birth

For example, 3rd February is entered as 0302

Centre Stamp

Instructions

Write your Examination Number and your Day and Month of Birth in the boxes on the front cover.

Write your answers to all parts of the examination into this answerbook. This answerbook will be scanned and your work will be presented to an examiner on screen. Anything that you write outside of the answer areas may not be seen by the examiner.

Write your answers in blue or black pen. You may use pencil for sketches, graphs and diagrams only.

There are three sections to this examination. Questions for **Sections B and C** are supplied separately but your answers must be written in this answerbook.

Section A	30 marks
Answer any **five** questions in this section.
Each question carries 6 marks.

Section B	130 marks
Answer **Question 1** and **one** question from questions 2, 3, 4 and 5.
Question 1 is worth 80 marks.
Questions 2, 3, 4 and 5 are worth 50 marks each.

Section C	40 or 80 marks
Answer **one** elective question **or** Question 4 (core), to include **part (a)** and either **part (b)** or **part (c)**.

If you submitted *Textiles, Fashion and Design* coursework for examination, you may only attempt Question 2 from this section.

Electives 1 and 3 are worth 80 marks each.
Elective 2 is worth 40 marks.
Question 4 (core) is worth 80 marks.

Section A 30 marks

Answer any **five** questions from this section.
Each question carries 6 marks.
Write your answers in the spaces provided.

1. State **two** functions of calcium in the body.

(i)

(ii)

Identify **one** factor that affects calcium absorption.

2. Complete the table below in relation to the digestion of carbohydrates.

Secretion	Enzyme	Substrate	Product
Pancreatic juice			

3. In relation to proteins, explain foam formation.

Give **one** culinary example of foam formation.

4. Describe how the chemical structure of cis fatty acids and trans fatty acids differ.

5. Outline **three** guidelines to follow to achieve a light pastry.

(i)

(ii)

(iii)

6. In relation to freezing, describe quick-freezing.

Give **one** advantage of quick-freezing.

7. State a different benefit of each of the following types of food packaging:

Food packaging	Benefit
Polystyrene	
Glass bottle	
Waxed carton	

8. Identify **one** moist method of cooking suitable for fish.

Describe the underlying principle of the cooking method named.

9. Outline the function of each of the following in relation to food additives:

Anti-caking agent
Emusifier

81

10. In relation to an individual's income, explain each of the following:

Pay Related Social Insurance (PRSI)
Universal Social Charge (USC)

11. Name **one** statutory consumer protection agency.

Outline the role of the statutory agency named.

12. Name **two** types of life assurance.

(i)
(ii)

Identify **one** difference between the two types of life assurance named.

13. State **two** pieces of information that should be found on a permanent label under the Fire Safety (Domestic Furniture) Order (1988, 1995).

(i)
(ii)

14. What information does each of the following symbols convey to the consumer?

Green dot
(*www.wikimedia.org*)

Eco label
(*www.therecycler.com*)

Answerbook for Sections B and C

Instructions

Questions for **Sections B** and **C** are supplied separately.

Start each question on a new page. Write the question number in the box at the top of each page. Use the left-hand column to label each part, as shown below.

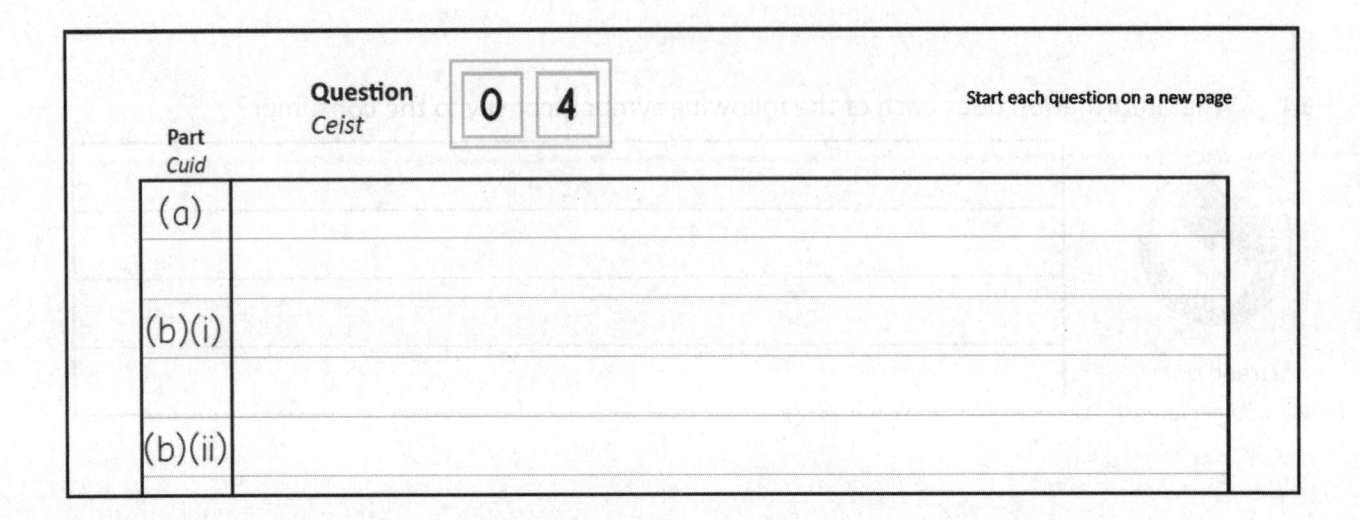

Part Cuid	Question Ceist	0 4	Start each question on a new page
(a)			
(b)(i)			
(b)(ii)			

You do not need to use all of the pages in this answerbook. If you run out of space in this answerbook, you may ask the superintendent for more paper.

Write your answers in blue or black pen. You may use pencil for sketches, graphs and diagrams only.

*New Format: From 2020 the returnable answerbook is provided with this section of the Exam Paper

Do not write on this page

Copyright notice
This examination paper may contain text or images for which the State Examinations Commission is not the copyright owner, and which may have been adapted, for the purpose of assessment, without the authors' prior consent. This examination paper has been prepared in accordance with *Section 53(5) of the Copyright and Related Rights Act, 2000*. Any subsequent use for a purpose other than the intended purpose is not authorised. The Commission does not accept liability for any infringement of third-party rights arising from unauthorised distribution or use of this examination paper.

Leaving Certificate – Higher Level

Home Economics – Scientific and Social
Section A and Answerbook

Wednesday 8 June
Afternoon 2:00 - 4:30

2022. M48

2022L098A2EL

Coimisiún na Scrúduithe Stáit
State Examinations Commission

LEAVING CERTIFICATE EXAMINATION 2022

Home Economics – Scientific and Social

HIGHER LEVEL

Section B and Section C

WEDNESDAY 8 JUNE   AFTERNOON 2:00 – 4:30

Section B   130 marks
Answer **Question 1** and **one** question from questions 2, 3, 4 and 5.
Question 1 is worth 80 marks.
Questions 2, 3, 4 and 5 are worth 50 marks each.

Section C   40 or 80 marks
Answer **one** elective question **or** Question 4 (core), to include **part (a)** and either **part (b)** or **part (c)**.

If you submitted *Textiles, Fashion and Design* coursework for examination, you may only attempt Question 2 from this section.

Electives 1 and 3 are worth 80 marks each.
Elective 2 is worth 40 marks.
Question 4 (core) is worth 80 marks.

Do not hand this up.
This document will not be returned to the
State Examinations Commission.

Section B — 130 marks

Answer **Question 1** and **one** question from questions 2, 3, 4 and 5.
Question 1 is worth 80 marks. Questions 2, 3, 4 and 5 are worth 50 marks each.
Write your answer in the answerbook containing **Section A**.

Question 1

'Health-related habits developed during teenage years tend to persist into adulthood.' (*iuna.net*)

The National Teens Food Survey II highlights the difficulties teenagers experience when trying to eat a healthy diet.
(*adapted from iuna.net*)

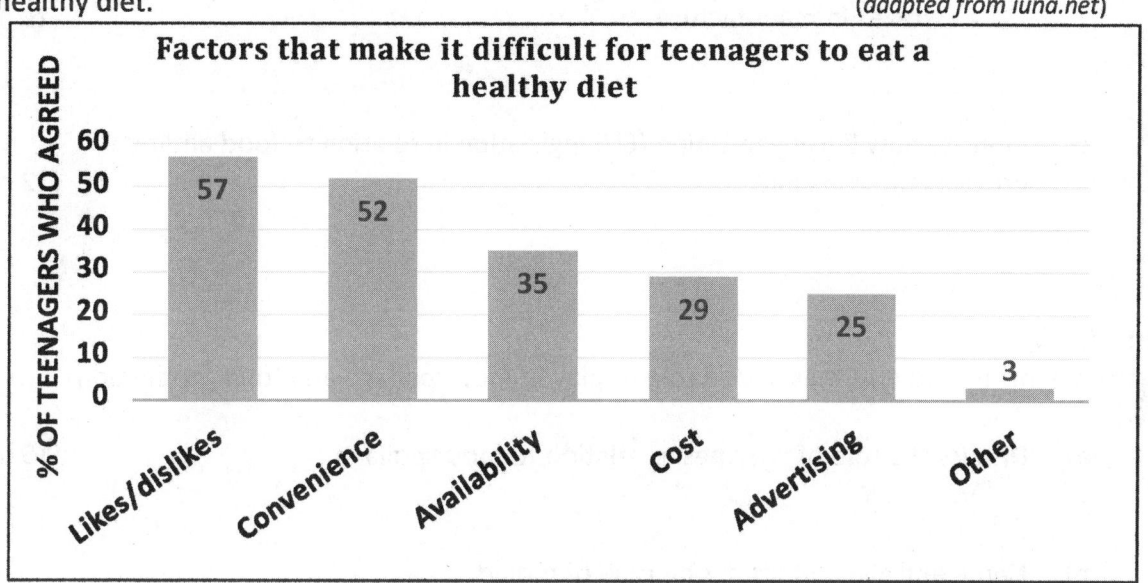

Factors that make it difficult for teenagers to eat a healthy diet
(% of teenagers who agreed)

- Likes/dislikes: 57
- Convenience: 52
- Availability: 35
- Cost: 29
- Advertising: 25
- Other: 3

(a) Using the information provided in the chart, comment and elaborate on the factors that make it difficult for teenagers to eat a healthy diet. (20 marks)

(b) Give a detailed account of the dietary measures to follow when planning and preparing meals for teenagers. (20 marks)

(c) An adequate intake of Vitamin D is essential in a healthy diet.

Give an account of Vitamin D with reference to:
- biological functions
- effects of deficiency
- properties. (20 marks)

(d) Discuss how the health status of an individual can influence their choice when purchasing foods. (20 marks)

Question 2
Vegan diets are increasing in popularity; however, these diets require careful planning.

    (a)   Identify **three** nutrients that could be deficient in a vegan diet and outline a strategy to prevent the deficiency of each nutrient.   (18 marks)

    (b)   Set out details of an alternative protein food you have studied.
            Refer to:
- name
- stages in manufacture.   (20 marks)

    (c)   Indicate how European Union (EU) legislation in relation to food additives protects the consumer.   (12 marks)

Question 3
Micro-organisms and enzymes have a role to play in food spoilage and food production.

    (a)   Discuss the role of enzymes in relation to food spoilage.   (15 marks)

    (b)   Name and give details of **one** type of mould.
            Refer to:
- name
- characteristics/description
- conditions necessary for growth.   (23 marks)

    (c)   Assess the uses of micro-organisms in food production.   (12 marks)

Question 4

'Homeownership is good for individuals, families and communities.' (*Housing for All, 2021*)

(a) Analyse the socio-economic factors that determine housing choices for potential buyers. (16 marks)

(b) Discuss the conditions that lending institutions require for potential buyers in order to qualify for a mortgage. (24 marks)

(c) Explain how consumers are protected by the Sale of Goods and Supply of Services Act (1980) when availing of the services of an electrician in the home. (10 marks)

Question 5

Marriage and families are recognised social structures.

(a) Describe the legal obligations for marriage in Ireland. (16 marks)

(b) Analyse how socio-economic factors have affected the changing roles of older family members in contemporary society. (20 marks)

(c) State why it is important to make a will and outline the procedure involved in making a will. (14 marks)

Section C
40 or 80 marks

Answer **one** elective question **or** Question 4 (core), to include **part (a)** and either **part (b) or (c)**.
If you submitted *Textiles, Fashion and Design* coursework for examination,
you may only attempt Question 2 from this section.
Write your answer in the answerbook containing **Section A**.

Elective 1 – Home Design and Management – 80 marks

Candidates selecting this elective must answer **1(a)** and either **1(b) or 1(c)**.

1.(a) 'Working from home in separate home offices can improve work-life balance.'
(The Irish Times, 2021)

   (i) Identify and describe **three** professional services that could assist individuals when modifying their home to include a home office space. (15 marks)

   (ii) Recommend a suitable floor covering that can be used in a home office. Refer to:
- name of floor covering
- factors to consider when selecting a floor covering
- properties. (20 marks)

   (iii) Outline how colour, pattern and texture can be used to enhance the interior design of a room. (15 marks)

and

1.(b) 'Proper ventilation is very important.' *(seai.ie)*

   (i) Describe the effects of poor ventilation in the home. (12 marks)

   (ii) Recommend **one** artificial method of ventilation suitable for a kitchen. Explain the underlying principle of this method. (18 marks)

or

1.(c) '25% of the energy used in Ireland is used in our homes.' *(seai.ie)*

   (i) Set out details of solar energy as an energy supply source to the home. Refer to:
- a system used in the home to utilise solar energy
- merits of using solar energy
- sustainability. (18 marks)

   (ii) Explain, giving an example, the underlying principle of a method of insulation used in the home. (12 marks)

Elective 2 – Textiles, Fashion and Design – 40 marks

Candidates selecting this elective must answer **2(a)** and either **2(b)** or **2(c)**.

2.(a) 'Smart casual is a fusion of two contrasting dress codes.' (*Louis Copeland*)

(*www.shutterstock.com*)

- (i) Evaluate the design of the outfits shown in the image above.
  Refer to:
    - comfort
    - aesthetic appeal
    - lifestyle. (15 marks)

- (ii) Discuss how colour can be used to flatter body size and shape. (10 marks)

and

2.(b)
- (i) Differentiate between regenerated and synthetic fibres. (6 marks)
- (ii) Explain filament modification, giving **two** examples. (9 marks)

or

2.(c) The functionality and aesthetic appeal of a garment has a strong influence on its design.

- (i) Describe **one** method of modifying a commercial pattern to tailor it to the specific needs of an individual. (9 marks)

- (ii) Discuss how traditional crafts have influenced Irish design and the fashion industry. (6 marks)

Elective 3 – Social Studies – 80 marks

Candidates selecting this elective must answer **3(a)** and either **3(b) or 3(c)**.

3.(a) According to CSO data, 216 959 people were estimated to be either out of work or in receipt of the government's pandemic unemployment payment in November 2021. (*www.cso.ie*)

   (i) Define unemployment. (6 marks)

   (ii) Discuss the following as contributory factors to unemployment in Ireland.
   Refer to:
   - changing requirements of industry
   - geographical location
   - level of consumer demand for products and services. (20 marks)

   (iii) Describe the effects of unemployment on society. (12 marks)

   (iv) Name **one** statutory initiative aimed at creating employment and outline how it helps to enhance employment options. (12 marks)

and

3.(b) 'Everyone has a right to rest and leisure.' (*UN, Universal Declaration of Human Rights*)

   (i) Analyse how young people benefit from participating in leisure activities. (12 marks)

   (ii) Name and evaluate **two** popular leisure facilities you have studied.
   Refer to:
   - cost and value for money
   - range of facilities offered. (18 marks)

or

3.(c) The Irish education system provides a holistic education for children.

   (i) Analyse the factors that influence the educational achievement of school children. (16 marks)

   (ii) Evaluate **two** initiatives aimed at providing equality of opportunity in education with reference to early school leavers. (14 marks)

Question 4 – Core – 80 marks

Candidates selecting this question must answer **4(a)** and either **4(b) or 4(c)**.

4.(a) 'Food waste is bad for the environment and bad for our pockets.' (*www.safefood.net*)

  (i) Discuss the nutritional significance of vegetables in the diet. (20 marks)

  (ii) Give an account of a method of home preservation suitable for vegetables.
  Refer to:
  - name of preservation method
  - underlying principle
  - suitable packaging. (18 marks)

  (iii) Evaluate irradiation as a commercial method of food preservation. (12 marks)

and

4.(b) 'Being on a restrictive diet should not mean a restricted food experience.' (*www.delicious.ie*)

  (i) Outline the dietary guidelines that should be followed by a person with coeliac disease. (15 marks)

  (ii) Analyse the growing popularity of speciality foods produced by small businesses in Ireland. (15 marks)

or

4.(c) Household technology has become an integral part of our lives.

  (i) Set out details of a study you have undertaken on an appliance with a heating element.
  Refer to:
  - construction
  - working principle
  - guidelines for use. (18 marks)

  (ii) Discuss the factors that influence consumers' decision making when purchasing large household appliances. (12 marks)

Leaving Certificate – Higher Level

Home Economics - Scientific and Social
Section B and Section C

Wednesday 8 June
Afternoon 2:00 – 4:30

2021.M48

Coimisiún na Scrúduithe Stáit
State Examinations Commission

Leaving Certificate Examination 2021
Home Economics – Scientific and Social

Section A and Answerbook

Higher Level

Wednesday 9 June   Afternoon 2:00 – 4:30

200 or 240 marks

Examination Number

Day and Month of Birth

For example, 3rd February is entered as 0302

Centre Stamp

Instructions

Write your Examination Number and your Day and Month of Birth in the boxes on the front cover.

Write your answers to all parts of the examination into this answerbook. This answerbook will be scanned and your work will be presented to an examiner on screen. Anything that you write outside of the answer areas may not be seen by the examiner.

Write your answers in blue or black pen. You may use pencil for sketches, graphs and diagrams only.

There are three sections to this examination. Questions for **Sections B and C** are supplied separately but your answers must be written in this answerbook.

Section A   30 marks
Answer any **five** questions in this section.
Each question carries 6 marks.

Section B   130 marks
Answer **Question 1** and **one** question from questions 2, 3, 4 and 5.
Question 1 is worth 80 marks.
Questions 2, 3, 4 and 5 are worth 50 marks each.

Section C   40 or 80 marks
Answer **one** elective question **or** question 4 (core) to include **part (a)** and either **part (b) or (c)**.

If you submitted *Textiles, Fashion and Design* coursework for examination, you may only attempt Question 2 from this section.

Electives 1 and 3 are worth 80 marks each.
Elective 2 is worth 40 marks.
Question 4 (core) is worth 80 marks.

Section A 30 marks

Answer any **five** questions from this section.
Each question carries 6 marks.
Write your answers in the spaces provided.

1. State **two** causes of protein denaturation and give **one** example in each case.

Cause	Example

2. In relation to lipids, explain each of the following:

Oxidative rancidity
Hydrolytic rancidity

3. Name **one** condition (disease) associated with a deficiency of the following nutrients:

Nutrient	Deficiency disease
Vitamin D	
Vitamin B_3 (Niacin)	
Iodine	

4. What is Basal Metabolic Rate (BMR)?

Give **two** factors that determine a person's basal metabolic rate.

(i)
(ii)

5. Name **three** properties of sugar and state **one** culinary use of each.

Property	Culinary use

6. Outline **two** benefits of incorporating frozen foods in meal planning.

(i)
(ii)

7. Explain the effect of each of the following in relation to the processing of vegetables and fruit:

Canning
Dehydration

8. Name **two** protein alternatives that can be used in a vegan diet.

(i)
(ii)

State **two** advantages of including protein alternatives in the diet.

(i)
(ii)

9. Explain the following chemical changes that occur during food preparation/cooking:

Enzymic browning
Non-enzymic browning

10. State the function of the following parts of the refrigerator:

the thermostat
the refrigerant

11. Classify **three** types of retail outlet and give **one** example in each class.

Type of retail outlet	Example

12. Outline **three** consumer responsibilities.

(i)
(ii)
(iii)

13. Identify **three** socio-economic factors that influence housing choices.

(i)
(ii)
(iii)

14. State **two** benefits of the small claims procedure.

(i)
(ii)

Answerbook for Sections B and C

Instructions

Questions for **Sections B** and **C** are supplied separately.

Start each question on a new page. Write the question number in the box at the top of each page. Use the left-hand column to label each part, as shown below.

Part Cuid	Question *Ceist*	0 4	Start each question on a new page *Cuir tús le gach ceist ar leathanach nua*
(a)			
(b)(i)			
(b)(ii)			

You do not need to use all of the pages in this answerbook. If you run out of space in this answerbook, you may ask the superintendent for more paper.

Write your answers in blue or black pen. You may use pencil for sketches, graphs and diagrams only.

---

*New Format: From 2020 the returnable answerbook is provided with this section of the Exam Paper

Do not write on this page

Copyright notice
This examination paper may contain text or images for which the State Examinations Commission is not the copyright owner, and which may have been adapted, for the purpose of assessment, without the authors' prior consent. This examination paper has been prepared in accordance with Section 53(5) of the Copyright and Related Rights Act, 2000. Any subsequent use for a purpose other than the intended purpose is not authorised. The Commission does not accept liability for any infringement of third-party rights arising from unauthorised distribution or use of this examination paper.

Leaving Certificate – Higher Level

Home Economics – Scientific and Social
Section A and Answerbook

Wednesday 9 June
Afternoon 2:00 – 4:30

2021. M48

2021L098A2EL

Coimisiún na Scrúduithe Stáit
State Examinations Commission

LEAVING CERTIFICATE EXAMINATION 2021

Home Economics – Scientific and Social

HIGHER LEVEL

Section B and Section C

WEDNESDAY 9 JUNE   AFTERNOON 2:00 – 4:30

Section B	130 marks Answer **Question 1** and **one** question from questions 2, 3, 4 and 5. Question 1 is worth 80 marks. Questions 2, 3, 4 and 5 are worth 50 marks each.
Section C	40 or 80 marks Answer **one** elective question **or** question 4 (core) to include **part (a)** and either **part (b) or (c)**. If you submitted *Textiles, Fashion and Design* coursework for examination, you may only attempt Question 2 from this section. Electives 1 and 3 are worth 80 marks each. Elective 2 is worth 40 marks. Question 4 (core) is worth 80 marks.

Do not hand this up

Section B
130 marks

Answer **Question 1** and **one** question from questions 2, 3, 4 and 5.
Question 1 is worth 80 marks. Questions 2, 3, 4 and 5 are worth 50 marks each.
Write your answer in the answerbook containing **Section A**.

Question 1
The following infographic shows two influencing factors on evening meal consumption.
(What Ireland Ate Last Night, Report 2020, Bord Bia Thinking House)

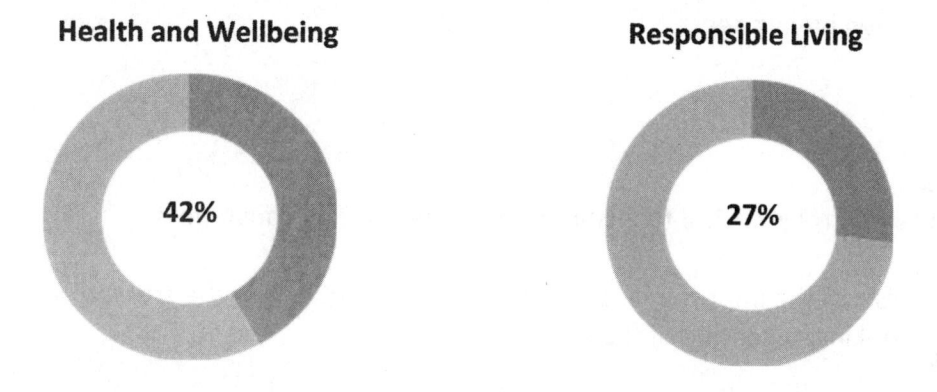

Health and Wellbeing — 42%

Responsible Living — 27%

(a) In relation to the infographic above, suggest how (i) health and wellbeing and (ii) responsible living might influence food choices. **(20 marks)**

(b) Identify and describe contemporary trends in Irish eating patterns. **(12 marks)**

(c) Micronutrients are essential for good health and wellbeing.

Give an account of iron with reference to:
- sources in the diet
- biological functions
- effects of deficiency. **(18 marks)**

(d) Identify and explain **two** factors which affect the absorption of iron in the body. **(10 marks)**

(e) Devise a set of strategies when purchasing foods and planning meals for families with irregular daily routines. **(20 marks)**

Question 2
Eggs are a good choice as part of a healthy, balanced diet.

(a) Discuss the nutritional significance of eggs in the diet. (20 marks)

(b) Describe how eggs work as an emulsifier in food production. Refer to **one** culinary application. (18 marks)

(c) Evaluate the role of food labelling as a source of consumer information when buying eggs. (12 marks)

Question 3
Temperature control is critical to ensuring food safety for all consumers.

(a) Discuss the importance of temperature control during the storage and cooking/reheating of food. (16 marks)

(b) Describe the stages in a *Hazard Analysis and Critical Control Point* (HACCP) system for making a hot main course dish. Refer to potential hazards and the corresponding control measures that should be implemented. (24 marks)

(c) Differentiate between infectious food poisoning and toxic food poisoning. (10 marks)

Question 4
Efficient home management guides the smooth running of the home.

  (a) Explain how good management systems contribute to a well-run home. (16 marks)

  (b) Using the management framework (inputs, throughputs and outputs), outline the strategies to be followed when planning a family holiday to ensure effective management of resources. (18 marks)

  (c) Evaluate the use of credit as a method of payment for a family holiday. (16 marks)

Question 5
The modern Irish family is smaller and more diverse than ever before.

  (a) Define the term 'family' and explain the concept of the universality of the family. (10 marks)

  (b) Explain how the family can meet the physical, emotional, economic and social needs of its members. (24 marks)

  (c) Discuss the challenges that may be experienced by the family of a child with special needs. (16 marks)

Section C

40 or 80 marks

Answer **one** elective question **or** question 4 (core) to include **part (a)** and either **part (b) or (c)**.
If you submitted *Textiles, Fashion and Design* coursework for examination,
you may only attempt Question 2 from this section.
Write your answer in the answerbook containing **Section A**.

Elective 1 – Home Design and Management – 80 marks

Candidates selecting this elective must answer **1(a)** and either **1(b)** or **1(c)**.

1.(a) A well designed home should have a positive impact on people's lives.

    (i) Explain the importance of location and house style when building a new home.
        (16 marks)

    (ii) Discuss the following factors that influence house design/construction:

- initial and/or maintenance costs
- technological developments
- energy efficiency.

        (24 marks)

    (iii) Outline the procedure involved in obtaining full planning permission to build a house.
        (10 marks)

and

1.(b) 'Lighting isn't just a practical necessity. It's a style accessory, too.' (*www.ikea.com*)

    (i) Discuss **three** properties of light and give an example of the application of each in the home.
        (18 marks)

    (ii) Identify and evaluate **two** contemporary developments in lighting technology.
        (12 marks)

or

1.(c) 'Water covers 71% of the planet but only 1% is available to us as drinking water.' (*Irish Water*)

    (i) Explain how water is supplied to and stored in the home.
    Refer to:

- urban or rural supply
- stopcock
- storage tank/cistern.

        (18 marks)

    (ii) Identify inefficient uses of water in the home. Suggest strategies for conserving and managing this resource.
        (12 marks)

Elective 2 – Textiles, Fashion and Design – 40 marks

Candidates selecting this elective must answer **2(a)** and either **2(b) or 2(c)**.

2.(a) *Athleisure* wear is a way of dressing that combines sportswear with ready-to-wear.

(www.pinterest.com)

    (i)   Evaluate the suitability of Athleisure wear as a wardrobe staple.   (15 marks)

    (ii)   Outline the steps of the design process when constructing a garment.   (10 marks)

and

2.(b) The sustainability of natural fibres has led to an upsurge in their use.

Write a profile of **one** fabric manufactured from natural fibres.
Refer to:
- fibre production
- fabric properties
- uses.   (15 marks)

or

2.(c) The design of fashion can be influenced by cultural, historical and social factors.

    (i)   Explain how the choice of clothing is determined by its function.   (6 marks)

    (ii)   Analyse the impact of social influences on the design of clothing.   (9 marks)

Elective 3 – Social Studies – 80 marks

Candidates selecting this elective must answer **3(a)** and either **3(b) or 3(c)**.

3.(a) 'Life on a low income is the norm for a large proportion of our society.'
(Poverty Focus, Social Justice Ireland, 2020)

    (i) Define poverty. (8 marks)

    (ii) In relation to poverty explain each of the following:
- relative poverty
- the poverty line
- the poverty trap. (18 marks)

    (iii) Discuss the extent and distribution of poverty in Ireland today. (12 marks)

    (iv) Name and give details of **one** social welfare assistance/benefit available to people who are experiencing poverty. (12 marks)

and

3.(b) People in work, paid or unpaid, tend to enjoy happier and healthier lives.

    (i) Identify and elaborate on the factors that affect an individual's attitude to work. (15 marks)

    (ii) Discuss giving examples, how a community can benefit from the work of volunteers. (15 marks)

or

3.(c) 42% of people who are working from home said that 'managing the boundary between work and home life was very difficult.' *(Irish Independent, 2020)*

    (i) Explain the importance of the distribution of work tasks and childcare responsibilities in families. (15 marks)

    (ii) Discuss how improvements in the provision of education have impacted on family life. (15 marks)

Question 4 – Core – 80 marks

Candidates selecting this elective must answer **4(a)** and either **4(b) or 4(c)**.

4.(a) 'Ireland has a population of less than five million people, yet it produces enough dairy to feed multiples of that.'   (*Dairy Sector Profile, Bord Bia*)

  (i) Discuss the nutritional significance of milk in the diet of young children. (20 marks)

  (ii) Describe **one** process used by manufacturers to extend the shelf life of milk. Refer to:
   - name of the process
   - how the process is carried out
   - packaging and labelling.   (18 marks)

  (iii) Outline the measures (initiatives) taken by the dairy industry to meet current consumer trends.   (12 marks)

and

4.(b) 'It is anticipated that the prevalence of diabetes in Ireland will increase to 278,000 by 2030.'   (*Changing Lives 2016 – 2020, Diabetes Ireland*)

  (i) In relation to diabetes, give an account of:
   - types of diabetes
   - dietary requirements that should be followed for individuals with diabetes.   (20 marks)

  (ii) Outline the uses of sweeteners in food production.   (10 marks)

or

4.(c) Market research involves the use of a variety of consumer research methods.

  (i) Name and describe **two** methods of consumer research.   (12 marks)

  (ii) Outline the benefits of consumer research for both the consumer and the retailer.   (18 marks)

Do not hand this up

Copyright notice
This examination paper may contain text or images for which the State Examinations Commission is not the copyright owner, and which may have been adapted, for the purpose of assessment, without the authors' prior consent. This examination paper has been prepared in accordance with Section 53(5) of the Copyright and Related Rights Act, 2000. Any subsequent use for a purpose other than the intended purpose is not authorised. The Commission does not accept liability for any infringement of third-party rights arising from unauthorised distribution or use of this examination paper.

Leaving Certificate – Higher Level

Home Economics - Scientific and Social
Section B and Section C

Wednesday 9 June
Afternoon 2:00 – 4:30

2020.M48

2020L098A1EL

Coimisiún na Scrúduithe Stáit
State Examinations Commission

Leaving Certificate Examination 2020
Home Economics – Scientific and Social

Section A and Answerbook
Higher Level
2 hours 30 minutes
280 or 320 marks

Examination Number

Day and Month of Birth

For example, 3rd February is entered as 0302

Centre Stamp

2020 HL

Instructions

Write your Examination Number and your Day and Month of Birth in the boxes on the front cover.

Write your answers to all parts of the examination into this answerbook. This answerbook will be scanned and your work will be presented to an examiner on screen. Anything that you write outside of the answer areas may not be seen by the examiner.

Write your answers in blue or black pen. You may use pencil for sketches, graphs and diagrams only.

There are three sections to this examination. Questions for **Sections B and C** are supplied separately but your answers must be written in this answerbook.

Section A	60 marks
	Answer **ten** questions in this section.
	Each question carries 6 marks.
Section B	180 marks
	Answer **Question 1** and any other **two** questions.
	Question 1 is worth 80 marks.
	Questions 2, 3, 4, and 5 are worth 50 marks each.
Section C	40 or 80 marks
	Answer **one** elective question, to include **part (a)** and either **part (b)** or **(c)**.

If you submitted *Textiles, Fashion and Design* coursework for examination, you may only attempt Question 2 from this section.

Electives 1 and 3 are worth 80 marks each.
Elective 2 is worth 40 marks.

Section A 60 marks

Answer any **ten** questions from this section.
Each question carries 6 marks.
Write your answers in the spaces provided.

1. Complete the following table in relation to carbohydrates.

	Chemical Formula	Example
Monosaccharides		
Disaccharides		
Polysaccharides		

2. Outline how consumers have become more nutritionally aware and health conscious in their food choices.

(i)

(ii)

3. State **two** functions of omega 3 fatty acids in the diet.

(i)

(ii)

4. The following health conditions may result from a vitamin deficiency in the diet. Identify **one** vitamin in each case.

Health Condition	Vitamin
Poor blood clotting	
Neural tube defects	
Night blindness	

5. State **two** functions of An Bord Bia (The Irish Food Board).

(i)

(ii)

6. In relation to meat, explain each of the following terms:

(i) Extractives

(ii) Marinating

7. Outline the process involved in the homogenisation of milk.

8. Classify artificial sweeteners and give **one** example in each class/type.

Class/Type	Example

9. What information does each of the following symbols convey to the consumer?

(www.repak.ie)

(www.clearpak.com)

10. In relation to fabric detergents, explain the purpose of each of the following:

(i) Enzymes

(ii) Surfactants

11. Differentiate between the mortgage interest rates below.

(i) Fixed rate

(ii) Variable rate

12. Describe how each of the following influence consumers when shopping.

(i) Product placement

(ii) Loyalty schemes

Answerbook for Sections B and C

Instructions

Questions for **Sections B** and **C** are supplied separately.

Start each question on a new page. Write the question number in the box at the top of each page. Use the left-hand column to label each part, as shown below.

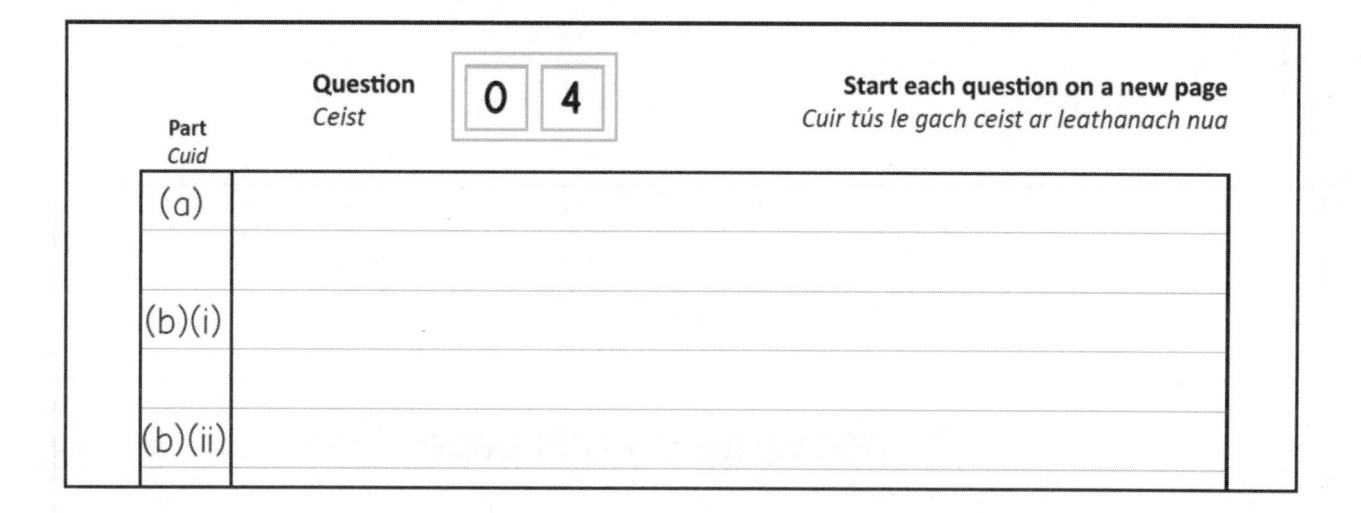

Part Cuid	Question *Ceist*	0 4	Start each question on a new page *Cuir tús le gach ceist ar leathanach nua*
(a)			
(b)(i)			
(b)(ii)			

You do not need to use all of the pages in this answerbook. If you run out of space in this answerbook, you may ask the superintendent for more paper.

Write your answers in blue or black pen. You may use pencil for sketches, graphs and diagrams only.

*New Format: From 2020 the returnable answerbook is provided with this section of the Exam Paper

2020 HL

Do not write on this page

Copyright notice
This examination paper may contain text or images for which the State Examinations Commission is not the copyright owner, and which may have been adapted, for the purpose of assessment, without the authors' prior consent. This examination paper has been prepared in accordance with Section 53(5) of the Copyright and Related Rights Act, 2000. Any subsequent use for a purpose other than the intended purpose is not authorised. The Commission does not accept liability for any infringement of third-party rights arising from unauthorised distribution or use of this examination paper.

Leaving Certificate – Higher Level

Home Economics – Scientific and Social
Section A and Answerbook

2 hours 30 minutes

2020. M48

2020L098A2EL

Coimisiún na Scrúduithe Stáit
State Examinations Commission

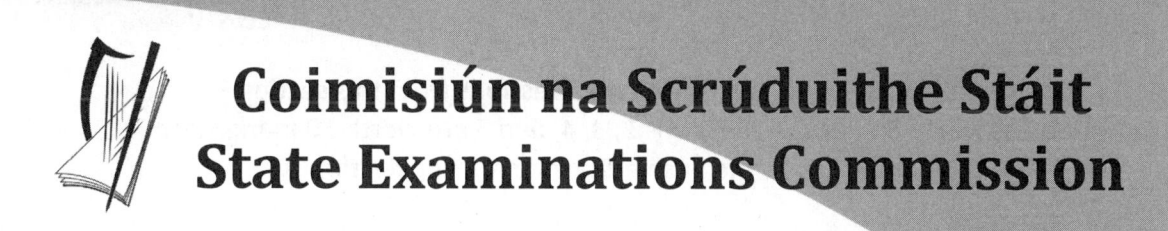

LEAVING CERTIFICATE EXAMINATION 2020

Home Economics – Scientific and Social

HIGHER LEVEL

Section B and Section C

2 hours 30 minutes

Section B 180 marks
Answer **Question 1** and any other **two** questions.
Question 1 is worth 80 marks.
Questions 2, 3, 4, and 5 are worth 50 marks each.

Section C 40 or 80 marks
Answer **one** elective question, to include **part (a)** and either part **(b)** or **(c)**.

If you submitted *Textiles, Fashion and Design* coursework for examination, you may only attempt Question 2 from this section.

Electives 1 and 3 are worth 80 marks each.
Elective 2 is worth 40 marks.

Do not hand this up

Section B
180 marks

Answer **Question 1** and any other **two questions** from this section.
Question 1 is worth 80 marks. Questions 2, 3, 4, and 5 are worth 50 marks each.
Write your answer in the answerbook containing **Section A**.

Question 1
Consumer surveys confirm that large portion sizes are associated with overeating in both adults and children. The following table from a study carried out by *safe*food reveals participants' opinions on situations where it is difficult to manage food portion sizes.

Situations/Settings	Sometimes Difficult (%)	Always Difficult (%)	Never Difficult (%)
Eating in	45	7.5	47.5
Eating out	57.5	10	32.5
Eating at work	20	0	80
Eating with friends	62.5	2.5	35
Stressful situations	35	10	55
Lack of time	40	2.5	57.5
Special occasions	40	37.5	22.5
Eating late/after a night out	35	7.5	57.5
Eating while watching TV	50	2.5	47.5
Preparing a meal	20	5	75

(*www.safefood.eu/media/safefoodlibrary*)

(a) With reference to **five** of the above situations/settings, suggest reasons why participants may/may not find it difficult to manage portion sizes. (20 marks)

(b) Give a detailed account of protein and refer to:
- how a peptide bond is formed
- essential and non-essential amino acids
- supplementary value/complementary role. (24 marks)

(c) Proteins have many functions in food production.
Explain the following in relation to protein and make reference to the culinary application of each:
- gel formation
- foam formation. (16 marks)

(d) Devise a set of strategies for controlling food portion sizes when shopping for food, eating at home and eating out. (20 marks)

Question 2
Cereal products such as bread, pasta and rice are significant energy providers for the body.

    (a)   Discuss the nutritional significance of cereals in the diet.   (20 marks)

    (b)   Outline the stages involved in the processing of a cereal product of your choice.
           In your answer refer to production, packaging and labelling.   (18 marks)

    (c)   Explain the benefits of a diet high in fibre.   (12 marks)

Question 3
Safe food storage and preparation practices help to prevent food waste and foodborne illnesses.

    (a)   Discuss methods of good practice to ensure the safe preparation and storage
           of food in the home.   (12 marks)

    (b)   Describe **two** methods of home food preservation.
           In each case refer to:
- how the method of preservation is carried out
- the underlying principle
- risk of food spoilage.   (26 marks)

    (c)   Outline the protection provided to the consumer by current food legislation.
           Refer to **one** Regulation/Act in your answer.   (12 marks)

Question 4
Design and style are inherent factors in modern kitchen appliances.

- (a) Name and describe **one** household appliance with a motor suitable for use in a kitchen. Refer to:
    - selection criteria
    - sourcing consumer information
    - working principle
    - guidelines for use. (26 marks)

- (b) Outline how the consumer can protect the environment when choosing, using and disposing of electrical appliances. (12 marks)

- (c) Explain how the Sale of Goods and Supply of Services Act (1980) supports the consumer should the product prove faulty. (12 marks)

Question 5
A family is two or more people who share goals and values, have long term commitments to one another and usually reside in the same dwelling.

- (a) Give an account of the historical development of the family in Ireland from the middle of the twentieth century to the present day. (20 marks)

- (b) Outline the roles and responsibilities of family members and explain how these roles evolve through the life cycle of the family. (18 marks)

- (c) Discuss the importance of good communication within the family. (12 marks)

Section C   40 or 80 marks

Answer **one elective question** from this section.
If you submitted *Textiles, Fashion and Design* coursework for examination,
you may only attempt Question 2 from this section.
Write your answer in the answerbook containing **Section A**.

Elective 1 – Home Design and Management – 80 marks

Candidates selecting this elective must answer **1(a) and either 1(b) or 1(c)**.

1.(a) Flexibility of space is critical to the success of today's homes.

- **(i)** Evaluate the suitability of open plan living spaces in house design. (16 marks)

- **(ii)** Discuss the factors that should be considered when planning the interior design of a home. (16 marks)

- **(iii)** Describe **three** principles of design and give an example of the application of each principle when designing an interior space. (18 marks)

and

1.(b) 'The average rent in Ireland is at an all-time high and the availability of houses to rent is at its lowest ever level.'   (*www.daft.ie 2019*)

- **(i)** Discuss the comparative costs for a young couple of buying versus renting a house. (16 marks)

- **(ii)** Name and give details of **one** housing scheme offered by Local Authorities. (14 marks)

or

1.(c) The heating system is integral to the overall design of a home.

- **(i)** Explain the factors that should be considered when choosing a heating system for a new house. (16 marks)

- **(ii)** Name and describe **one** type of home central heating system.
  In your answer refer to:
    - fuel/energy source
    - working principle
    - impact on the environment. (14 marks)

Elective 2 – Textiles, Fashion and Design – 40 marks

Candidates selecting this elective must answer **2(a) and either 2(b) or 2(c)**.

2.(a) Style is the way to say who you are without having to speak.

  (i) Sketch and describe a daywear outfit suitable for a college student. (10 marks)

  (ii) Evaluate the outfit with reference to each of the following:
  - suitability for purpose
  - sustainability
  - current fashion trends. (15 marks)

and

2.(b) Fabrics are given a variety of treatments to alter their performance.

  (i) Identify **three** functional finishes applied to fabrics. (6 marks)

  (ii) Explain how finishes enhance fabric performance. (9 marks)

or

2.(c) The clothing and textile industry in Ireland provides significant employment.

  (i) Give a brief overview of the structure of the clothing and textile industry. (9 marks)

  (ii) Describe the importance of small businesses in this industry. (6 marks)

Elective 3 – Social Studies – 80 marks

Candidates selecting this elective must answer **3(a) and either 3(b) or 3(c)**.

3.(a) Education opens the minds of students and prepares them to face the world.

   (i) Explain how education is used as a method of socialisation for young children.

        (15 marks)

   (ii) Discuss the role of education in contributing to the development of the individual.
Refer to:
- physical development
- emotional development
- moral development
- intellectual development.

        (20 marks)

   (iii) Give an account of the supports provided in second level schools for children with special educational needs.

        (15 marks)

and

3.(b) 'The number of people unemployed in Ireland was 126,900 in September 2019.'
(*www.irish examiner.ie*)

   (i) Discuss the causes of unemployment. (9 marks)

   (ii) Outline the effects of unemployment on society. (12 marks)

   (iii) Name and give details of **one** statutory initiative that encourages foreign investment and creates employment. (9 marks)

or

3.(c) Leisure and sports activities play an important role in communities.

   (i) Describe how age and gender impact on a person's choice of leisure activities.

        (12 marks)

   (ii) Evaluate **two** leisure facilities available in the community.
Refer to:
- facilities offered
- value for money
- benefit to the community.

        (18 marks)

Do not hand this up

Copyright notice
This examination paper may contain text or images for which the State Examinations Commission is not the copyright owner, and which may have been adapted, for the purpose of assessment, without the authors' prior consent. This examination paper has been prepared in accordance with Section 53(5) of the Copyright and Related Rights Act, 2000. Any subsequent use for a purpose other than the intended purpose is not authorised. The Commission does not accept liability for any infringement of third-party rights arising from unauthorised distribution or use of this examination paper.

Leaving Certificate – Higher Level

Home Economics - Scientific and Social
Section B and Section C

2 hours 30 minutes

2019. M48

2019L098A1EL

Write your Examination Number here

Coimisiún na Scrúduithe Stáit
State Examinations Commission

Leaving Certificate Examination, 2019

HOME ECONOMICS – SCIENTIFIC AND SOCIAL

HIGHER LEVEL

CENTRE STAMP

WEDNESDAY, 5 JUNE – AFTERNOON 2:00 to 4:30

280/320 MARKS

Instructions to Candidates

Section A There are **twelve questions** in this section.
Answer any **ten questions**.
Each question carries **6 marks**.
Write your answers in the spaces provided on the examination paper.

Section B There are **five questions** in this section.
Answer **Question 1 and any other two questions**.
Question 1 is worth **80 marks**.
Questions 2, 3, 4 and **5** are worth **50 marks** each.
Write your answers in the separate answer book provided.

Section C There are **three questions** in this section.
Answer **one** elective question, to include **part (a)** and either **part (b)** or **part (c)**.

If you submitted *Textiles, Fashion and Design* coursework for examination, you may only attempt Question 2 from this section.

Electives 1 and **3** are worth **80 marks** each. **Elective 2** is worth **40 marks**.

Write your answers in the separate answer book provided.

You must return this examination paper with your answer book at the end of the examination.

Section A

Answer any **ten** questions from this section.
Each question is worth 6 marks.
Write your answers in the spaces provided.

1. In relation to lipids, explain each of the following properties: (6)

   Hydrogenation _____

   _____

   _____

   Plasticity _____

   _____

   _____

2. Suggest **three** meal planning guidelines that should be considered when preparing meals for a person with Coronary Heart Disease (CHD). (6)

   (i) _____

   _____

   (ii) _____

   _____

   (iii) _____

   _____

3. Health conditions can result from a mineral deficiency in the diet.
   Identify **one** mineral in each case. (6)

Health Condition	Mineral
Osteomalacia	
Dry, flaky skin	
Goitre	

4. In relation to eggs, explain each of the following: (6)

Organic _____

_____

_____

Lecithin _____

_____

_____

5. Differentiate between each of the following methods of smoking fish. (6)

Cold smoking _____

_____

_____

Hot smoking _____

_____

_____

6. Describe **one** physical and **one** chemical change that occur during the cooking of food. (6)

Physical change _____

_____

_____

Chemical change _____

_____

_____

7. State **three** biological functions of water. (6)

(i) _____

(ii) _____

(iii) _____

8. Explain each of the following types of diabetes. (6)

Type 1: Insulin dependent _____

_____

_____

Type 2: Non-insulin dependent _____

_____

_____

9. Name **three** statutory bodies concerned with consumer protection. (6)

(i) _____

(ii) _____

(iii) _____

10. Outline the function of each of the following parts of a microwave oven. (6)

Magnetron _____

_____

_____

Transformer _____

_____

_____

11. In relation to the environment, explain and give an example of each of the following: (6)

Renewable resource _____

_____

_____

Example _____

Non-renewable resource _____

_____

_____

Example _____

12. Explain how consumers can contribute to sustainable waste management. (6)

(i) _____

_____

_____

(ii) _____

_____

_____

133

Section B

Answer **Question 1** and any other **two questions** from this section.
Question 1 is worth 80 marks. Questions 2, 3, 4 and 5 are worth 50 marks each.

1. Over 70% of all consumers snack each day. The following question was asked in a survey on snacking trends:

   "When choosing a snack for health benefits, which of the following are important to you?"

   The results of the survey question are given below.

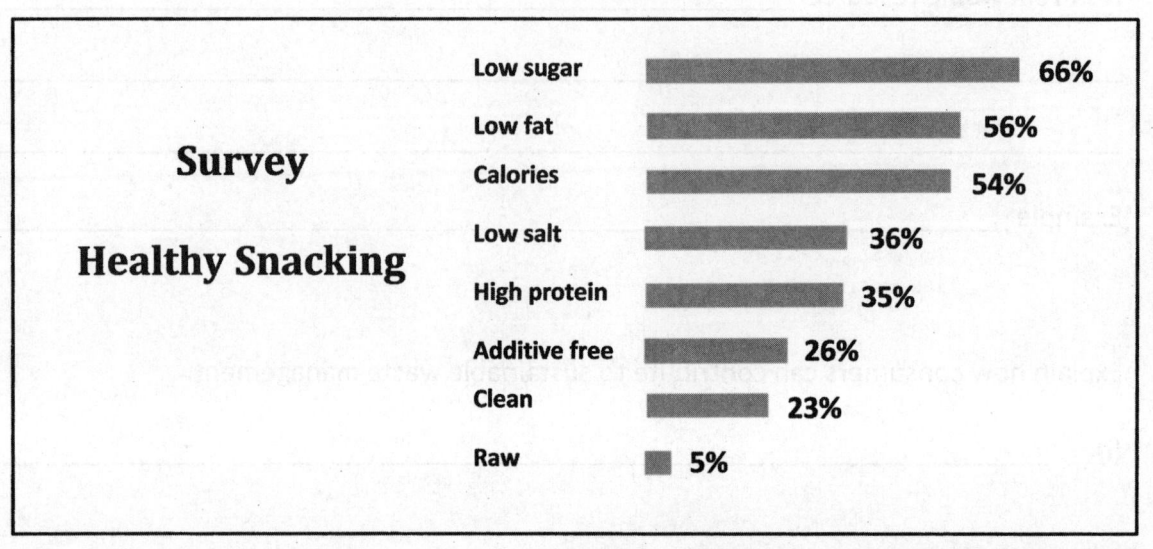

   Survey Healthy Snacking

Low sugar	66%
Low fat	56%
Calories	54%
Low salt	36%
High protein	35%
Additive free	26%
Clean	23%
Raw	5%

   (*Bord Bia - Healthy Snacking UK and Ireland, 2018*)

   (a) In addition to the benefits in the chart above what are the key factors that influence food choices? (12)

   (b) Discuss the motivations for the respondent choices given in the survey. (12)
   In your answer refer to **four** benefits.

   (c) Describe **two** healthy snacks suitable for college students.
   Outline the nutritional merits of incorporating these snacks in a person's diet. (18)

   (d) Dairy based snacks can contribute to micro-nutrient intake.
   Give an account of calcium under each of the following headings:
   - sources
   - biological functions
   - effects of deficiency. (18)

   (e) Explain how the packaging on food products attracts and informs consumers. (20)

2. 'Research reveals that 19% of the average weekly family food shop is spent on highly processed 'treat' foods. This compares with only 10% spent on fruit and 7% on vegetables.'

(Courtesy of www.safefoods.eu)

    (a) Discuss the nutritional significance of vegetables in the diet. (15)

    (b) **(i)** Suggest strategies for increasing a person's daily consumption of vegetables.

        (ii) Compile a set of guidelines for cooking vegetables in order to maintain their nutritive value. (20)

    (c) Give an account of Vitamin C (ascorbic acid) under each of the following headings:
- properties
- sources
- biological functions. (15)

3. Food spoilage is a disagreeable change in a food's normal state. Such changes can be detected by smell, taste, touch or sight.

    (a) Discuss the main causes of food spoilage. (20)

    (b) Name and give details of **one** common food poisoning bacteria.
Refer to:
- conditions necessary for growth
- source
- reproduction/growth of bacteria
- high risk foods. (20)

    (c) Outline the role of the Health Service Executive (HSE) in relation to food safety. (10)

4. 'The average gross weekly household income in 2016 was €1,100 which is 7% higher than the figure recorded for 2010.' *(Household Budget Survey, 2016)*

    (a) Analyse the factors that affect household income. (20)

    (b) Suggest strategies that should be followed when planning a family budget to ensure the effective management of financial resources. (20)

    (c) Outline the role of the Money Advice and Budgeting Service (MABS) for families who are experiencing financial difficulties. (10)

5. Sociology is the study of society, patterns of social relationships, social interaction and culture of everyday life.

    (a) Explain the following sociological terms:
- socialisation
- socio-economic group
- social mobility
- social change
- kinship. (14)

    (b) Describe the characteristics of contemporary family structures. (12)

    (c) Discuss the social, economic and technological changes that affect families today. (24)

Section C

Answer **one elective question** from this section.
If you submitted *Textiles, Fashion and Design* coursework for examination, you may **only** attempt **Question 2** from this section.

Elective 1 - Home Design and Management (80 marks)
Candidates selecting this elective must answer **1(a) and either 1(b) or 1(c)**.

1.(a) Architecture involves creating design solutions to make homes that meet the needs of the people who will live there.

    (i) Outline the historical development of housing styles in Ireland. (20)

    (ii) Discuss the economic and environmental factors that influence the choice of housing styles. (18)

    (iii) Give details of the professional services available to consumers to assist in the design and building of a home. (12)

and

1.(b) Walls can be a decorative feature, or may simply be background.

    (i) Outline **four** factors that should be considered when selecting wall finishes for a home. (16)

    (ii) Name and describe **two** types of wall finishes suitable for a kitchen/living room. State **two** properties of each finish. (14)

or

1.(c) 'Electricity is so much part of modern living that we can often take it for granted. It is a powerful and versatile energy but can be dangerous if not used properly.'
(www.esbnetworks.ie)

    (i) In relation to household electricity supply describe each of the following:
- ring circuit
- minature circuit breaker (MCB). (12)

    (ii) Compile a set of guidelines for the safe use of electricity in the home. (18)

Elective 2 - Textiles, Fashion and Design (40 marks)

Candidates selecting this elective must answer **2(a) and either 2(b) or 2(c)**.

2.(a) The growth of young people's spending power has ensured that the teenage market is a crucial sector of the fashion business.

    (i) Summarise the factors that influence teenagers when purchasing clothes. (15)

    (ii) Sketch and describe an outfit suitable to wear to an outdoor music festival. (10)

and

2.(b) A fabric's appearance, properties and end use is influenced by the way it is constructed.

    (i) Explain how knitted fabric is constructed. (9)

    (ii) Outline the properties and uses of knitted fabric. (6)

or

2.(c) Talented young designers ensure that the Irish fashion industry continues to thrive.

    (i) Elaborate on the work of a contemporary Irish fashion designer. (6)

    (ii) Explain how the economy influences the design and fashion industry. (9)

Elective 3 - Social Studies (80 marks)

Candidates selecting this elective must answer **3(a) and either 3(b) or 3(c)**.

3.(a) 'Central Statistics Office (CSO) statistics, show the employment rate is up 3% so far this year. Almost 2.3 million people in Ireland are now in work.' (*Irish Examiner, November 2018*)

   (i) In relation to the food industry, comment on the contribution made by the primary, secondary and tertiary sectors. (12)

   (ii) Analyse the positive and negative effects of technology on work and employment. (16)

   (iii) Discuss how educational qualifications can lead to greater employment options. (10)

   (iv) Explain, giving examples, how legislation protects people in employment. (12)

and

3.(b) Quality childcare fulfils an important role for society.

   (i) Summarise the principal factors that influence a family's requirements for childcare. (12)

   (ii) Evaluate **two** different childcare options available to parents. (18)

or

3.(c) 'Over one in six people in Ireland are at risk of poverty and 105,051 people living in poverty in Ireland are actually in employment.' (*Central Statistics Office, 2017*)

   (i) Identify and discuss the groups of people who are at risk of poverty. Give reasons for your answer. (12)

   (ii) Discuss the influence of social policy on poverty. Include reference to how the state has responded to eliminating poverty. (18)

Write your Examination Number here   2018. M48

Coimisiún na Scrúduithe Stáit
State Examinations Commission

Leaving Certificate Examination, 2018

HOME ECONOMICS – SCIENTIFIC AND SOCIAL

HIGHER LEVEL

CENTRE STAMP

WEDNESDAY, 6 JUNE – AFTERNOON 2:00 to 4:30

280/320 MARKS

Instructions to Candidates

Section A There are **twelve questions** in this section.
Answer any **ten questions**.
Each question carries **6 marks**.
Write your answers in the spaces provided on the examination paper.

Section B There are **five questions** in this section.
Answer **Question 1 and any other two questions**.
Question 1 is worth **80 marks**.
Questions **2, 3, 4** and **5** are worth **50 marks** each.
Write your answers in the separate answer book provided.

Section C There are **three questions** in this section.
Answer **one** elective question, to include **part (a)** and either **part (b)** or **part (c)**.

If you submitted *Textiles, Fashion and Design* coursework for examination, you may only attempt Question 2 from this section.

Electives 1 and **3** are worth **80 marks** each. **Elective 2** is worth **40 marks**.

Write your answers in the separate answer book provided.

You must return this examination paper with your answer book at the end of the examination.

Section A

Answer any **ten** questions from this section.
Each question is worth 6 marks.
Write your answers in the spaces provided.

1. Complete the table below in relation to the digestion of carbohydrates. (6)

Organ	Enzyme	Substrate	Product
Pancreas			
Small Intestine			

2. State **three** functions of Vitamin C in the body. (6)

   (i) _____

   (ii) _____

   (iii) _____

3. Name **two** proteins found in meat. (6)

   (i) _____ (ii) _____

   Outline **two** effects of cooking on protein in meat.

   (i) _____

   (ii) _____

4. Outline the role of energy in the body. (6)

(i) _____

_____

(ii) _____

_____

(iii) _____

_____

5. Explain the significance of the following symbol to the consumer. (6)

_____

_____

_____

Name **two** products that use this symbol on their labelling.

(i) _____ (ii) _____

6. Complete the table below in relation to processed food.
Give **one** example of a different food / product in each case. (6)

	Food / Product
Foods that are extensively processed	
Foods processed to extend shelf life	
Fortified foods	

7. Explain **each** of the following methods of heat transfer when cooking food. (6)

Conduction _____

_____

_____

Convection _____

_____

_____

8. State the temperature range for optimum growth for **each** of the following groups of micro-organisms. (6)

Psychrophiles	
Mesophiles	
Thermophiles	

9. Suggest **two** textiles suitable for use in the home and state **one** property of each. (6)

Textile	Property

Name **one** fire retardant finish used on household textiles.

_____

10. Explain how advertising affects consumers' buying behaviour. (6)

(i) _____

_____

(ii) _____

_____

11. State **two** advantages of regular saving. (6)

(i) _____

_____

(ii) _____

_____

Name **two** saving schemes offered by financial institutions.

(i) _____   (ii) _____

12. In relation to a person's income, explain **each** of the following: (6)

Tax Credit _____

_____

USC _____

_____

Section B

Answer **Question 1** and any other **two questions** from this section.
Question 1 is worth 80 marks. Questions 2, 3, 4 and 5 are worth 50 marks each.

1. Calorie menu labelling in restaurants can help combat obesity even where only modest changes occur in consumer behaviour. *(Calories on menus in Ireland, FSAI)*

   Sample Main Course Menu

Grilled Irish Salmon	Chicken Tikka Masala	Beer Battered Fish & Chips
Irish salmon steak with pepper or basil butter or sticky honey, lime & chilli. Served with baby potatoes & peas.	Creamy tikka masala sauce over marinated chicken breast. Served with basmati rice, naan bread, mango chutney & poppadoms.	Fresh beer battered fish. Served with chips, mushy peas, lemon & tartare sauce.
387 calories	**883 calories**	**880 calories**
Chilli Con Carne	**Roast Vegetable Pasta**	**Fish Pie**
Irish beef mince chilli. Served with basmati rice & tortilla chips.	Tomatoes, courgettes and peppers in a tomato sauce over penne pasta, finished with cheddar cheese. Served with garlic bread.	White fish, smoked haddock & salmon in a creamy white sauce topped with mashed potatoes & cheese. Served with fresh bread.
662 calories	**747 calories**	**756 calories**

   (a) With reference to the sample menu above, comment and elaborate on the suitability of the menu options for a person on a weight reducing diet.
   In your answer, suggest modifications to the dishes for a healthier menu. (24)

   (b) In relation to lipids, state the elemental composition **and** describe the chemical structure of a triglyceride. (9)

   (c) Describe the structure and give **one** example of **each** of the following:
   - saturated fatty acids
   - monounsaturated fatty acids
   - polyunsaturated fatty acids. (18)

   (d) Outline the significance of fatty acids in the diet. (9)

   (e) The aim of food labelling is to provide consumers with information which may influence their purchasing decisions.

   In addition to nutritional information, discuss the reasons why consumers consult food labels on pre-packaged food prior to purchase. (20)

2. Vegetarian diets are a popular choice with many individuals and families.

   (a) In relation to vegetarian diets discuss:
   - classes / types
   - specific dietary requirements
   - benefits of a vegetarian diet. (30)

   (b) Name and describe **two** novel (alternative) protein foods that can be used in vegetarian diets. (8)

   (c) Outline the manufacture / production of **one** novel (alternative) protein food. (12)

3. Many modern processed products such as low calorie, snack and ready to eat convenience foods, would not be possible without the use of food additives.

   (a) What is a processed food?
   Evaluate the merits of incorporating processed foods in the diet. (20)

   (b) Give an informative account of flavourings **and** antioxidants.
   Refer to:
   - classes / types
   - examples
   - functions
   - use. (20)

   (c) Explain how the use of food additives is regulated by European Union (EU) legislation. (10)

4. Smart home technology is the automation and management of your home and daily life.

    (a) Discuss how technology has contributed to the efficient management of the home. (20)

    (b) Set out details of a study that you have undertaken on a refrigeration appliance. Refer to:
- working principle
- guidelines for use
- modern features. (22)

    (c) Evaluate the role of energy labelling when selecting household appliances. (8)

5. 'There can be no keener revelation of a society's soul than the way in which it treats its children'. *(Nelson Mandela)*

    (a) Identify and explain the rights of children in society today. (16)

    (b) Discuss the possible causes of conflict between adolescents and adults. Suggest strategies for resolving this conflict. (24)

    (c) Outline the protection available for families under the Family Law (Maintenance of Spouses and Children) Act, 1976. (10)

Section C

Answer **one elective question** from this section.
If you submitted *Textiles, Fashion and Design* coursework for examination,
you may **only** attempt **Question 2** from this section.

Elective 1 – Home Design and Management (80 marks)
Candidates selecting this elective must answer **1(a)** and either **1(b)** or **1(c)**.

1.(a) According to CSO figures, 896 families were homeless on census night including 1,726 children in those families. *(Central Statistics Office, 2016)*

    (i) Outline the housing requirements necessary to meet the needs of people who are homeless. (16)

    (ii) Give an informative account of the quality of accommodation provided in **each** of the following housing sectors:

- private housing sector / owner occupied
- private rental sector. (18)

    (iii) Discuss the importance of house building standards with reference to how building standards are regulated. (16)

and

1.(b) Well-chosen floor coverings provide style and beauty and improve the aesthetics of a room.

    (i) Outline **four** factors that should be considered when selecting floor coverings for a home. (12)

    (ii) Describe **three** types of flooring / floor coverings used in the home. List the properties of **each**. (18)

or

1.(c) Sustainable energy improves people's lives, brings comfort and convenience and addresses environmental challenges. *(Sustainable Energy Authority of Ireland)*

    (i) Identify and elaborate on **three** sources of energy supply to the home. Comment on the sustainability of **each** of these energy sources. (15)

    (ii) Give an account of the emissions produced from burning fuels in the home **and** the effect these emissions have on the environment. (15)

Elective 2 – Textiles, Fashion and Design (40 marks)

Candidates selecting this elective must answer **2(a)** and either **2(b)** or **2(c)**.

2.(a) 'Fashion is a trend, style lives within a person.' (*Oscar de la Renta*)

(*Adored Vintage: Runway Report/Sonia Rykiel*)

- **(i)** Assess the role of fashion as an expression of personality, with reference to the picture above. (15)

- **(ii)** Analyse the technological influences on the design and construction of clothing. (10)

and

2.(b) Natural fibres are a sustainable resource as they can be used without depleting or damaging the environment.

- **(i)** Classify natural fibres, giving examples **and** uses in each case. (9)

- **(ii)** Explain how fibres can be identified using a burning test.
  Give **one** example. (6)

or

2.(c) A commercial pattern reflects the designer's vision for the outfit.

- **(i)** Suggest reasons why commercial patterns may require modification. (9)

- **(ii)** Describe **one** method of modification to a commercial pattern. (6)

Elective 3 – Social Studies (80 marks)

Candidates selecting this elective must answer **3(a) and either 3(b) or 3(c)**.

3.(a) The demand for education is growing. Adults with higher educational attainment have better economic outcomes. *(Education at a Glance 2017, OECD)*

  (i) Name and describe **two** programmes provided in second level education. Refer to:
  - curriculum offered
  - assessment / examination system. (20)

  (ii) Analyse the factors that influence educational achievement. (15)

  (iii) Evaluate equality of opportunity in second level education with reference to students at risk of disadvantage and social exclusion. (15)

and

3.(b) Volunteering enriches individuals' lives and the communities in which they live.

  (i) Discuss, with examples, how a community can benefit from the work of volunteers. (15)

  (ii) Explain how a volunteer can benefit personally by participating in community projects. (15)

or

3.(c) Leisure is an important component of daily life and a core ingredient for overall well-being.

  (i) Discuss the value of leisure in today's society. (15)

  (ii) Analyse the social and cultural factors that influence an individual's choice of leisure activities. (15)

Write your Examination Number here　　　　　　　　　　　2017. M48

Coimisiún na Scrúduithe Stáit
State Examinations Commission

Leaving Certificate Examination, 2017

HOME ECONOMICS – SCIENTIFIC AND SOCIAL

HIGHER LEVEL

CENTRE STAMP

WEDNESDAY, 7 JUNE – AFTERNOON, 2.00 to 4.30

280/320 MARKS

Instructions to Candidates

Section A　There are **twelve** questions in this section.
Candidates are required to answer any **ten** questions.
Each question carries **6** marks.
Write your answers in the spaces provided on the examination paper.

Section B　There are **five** questions in this section.
Candidates are required to answer **Question 1 and any other two questions.**
Question 1 is worth **80** marks.
Questions 2, 3, 4 and **5** are worth **50** marks each.
Write your answers in the separate answer book provided.

Section C　There are **three** questions in this section.
Candidates are required to answer **one** elective question to include
part (a) and either **part (b)** or **part (c)**.
Candidates who submitted Textiles, Fashion and Design coursework for examination may only attempt Elective Question 2 from this section.
Electives **1** and **3** are worth **80** marks each. Elective **2** is worth **40** marks.
Write your answers in the separate answer book provided.

You must return your examination paper with your answer book at the end of the examination.

Section A

Answer any **ten** questions from this section.
Each question is worth 6 marks.
Write your answers in the spaces provided.

1. Amino acids are the building blocks of protein. (6)
   Explain **and** give an example of **each** of the following terms:

   Essential amino acids_____

   _____

   _____

   Example_____

   Non-essential amino acids_____

   _____

   _____

   Example_____

2. Describe the effect of gelatinisation on starch. (6)

   _____

   _____

   _____

   Give two culinary examples of gelatinisation.

   (i) _____ (ii) _____

3. Outline the role of the Food Safety Authority of Ireland (FSAI) in the food industry. (6)

   _____

   _____

   _____

152

4. Complete the following table in relation to anaemia. (6)

Cause	
Effect of deficiency	
Corrective measure	

5. Explain **each** of the following: (6)

Modified atmosphere packaging _____

_____

_____

Biodegradable packaging _____

_____

_____

6. Name **and** describe **two** common food poisoning bacteria using the headings below. (6)

Food poisoning bacteria	Description / characteristic	Habitat

7. Explain the process of *fermentation*. (6)

_____

_____

Name **two** by-products of fermentation.

(i) _____ (ii) _____

8. Complete the table below in relation to the processing of milk. (6)

Process	Temperature	Time	Effect
Ultra Heat Treatment			

9. Name **three** components / stages in family resource management. (6)

_____

_____

_____

Give **two** examples of family life which require management skills.

(i) _____

(ii) _____

10. Explain **each** of the following: (6)

Insurance premium _____

_____

Insurance policy _____

_____

11. Name **three** social welfare payments available to individuals. (6)

(i) _____

(ii) _____

(iii) _____

12. What protection is provided to the consumer by the Consumer Information Act, 1978 / Consumer Protection Act, 2007? (6)

(i) _____

_____

(ii) _____

_____

Section B

Answer **Question 1** and any other **two questions** from this section.
Question 1 is worth 80 marks. Questions 2, 3, 4 and 5 are worth 50 marks each.

1. **Rising levels of overweight and obesity are placing an increasing burden on individuals and society. Currently, six in ten adults and one in four children are overweight or obese.**

    (*A Healthy Weight for Ireland: Obesity Policy and Action Plan 2016 – 2025*)

    Body Mass Index (BMI) is a standardised measure used to estimate whether or not someone is underweight, normal weight, overweight or obese.

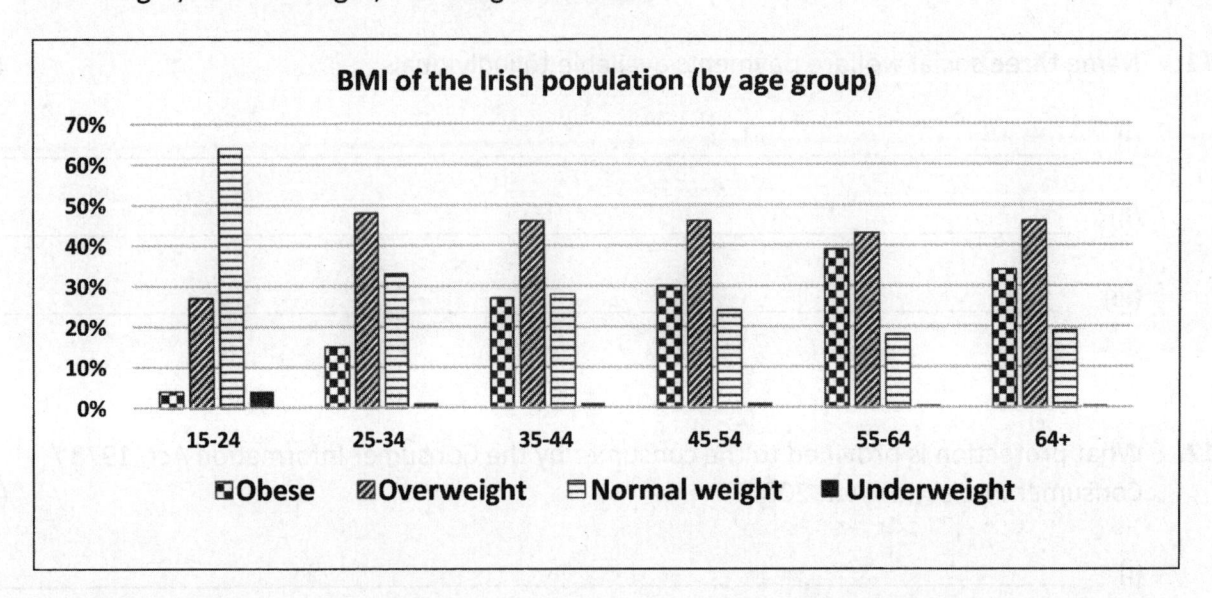

    BMI of the Irish population (by age group)

    (Bar chart showing percentages of Obese, Overweight, Normal weight, and Underweight across age groups 15-24, 25-34, 35-44, 45-54, 55-64, 64+)

    (a) Using the information provided in the chart, comment and elaborate on the variations in Body Mass Index among the different age groups of the Irish population. (20)

    (b) Classify *carbohydrates*.
    With reference to **each** class give:
    - the chemical formula
    - examples
    - food source. (15)

    (c) Explain **three** properties of sugar and the related culinary use of each. (15)

    (d) Assess the effects of high sugar consumption on the body. (10)

    (e) **The rate of obesity in Ireland has been increasing despite the fact that it is preventable.**
    Outline **five** strategies to be considered when purchasing **and** preparing food in order to reduce sugar consumption. (20)

2. **Ireland produces more farmhouse cheese varieties per capita than any other country in the world. Our reputation for quality extends overseas, with Ireland exporting 90% of the cheese it produces.**
   (The National Dairy Council)

   (a) Evaluate the nutritional value **and** the dietetic contribution of cheese to the diet. (20)

   (b) Describe the production of cheese.
   Refer to:
   - stages of production
   - packaging and labelling. (18)

   (c) Discuss the role of artisan producers / small businesses in the Irish food industry. (12)

3. **The 'taste' experience is an accumulation of multiple senses.**

   (a) Discuss the influence of the senses when choosing, cooking and eating food. (16)

   (b) Outline **four** conditions required for sensory analysis testing. (16)

   (c) Write a detailed account of **one** *difference test* used in the food industry.
   Refer to:
   - name of test
   - aim
   - implementation. (18)

4. **Everyone needs a home: a secure, comfortable place in a pleasant and sustainable community; a place to rear a family if they so wish and to grow old in serenity.**
   (*Social Housing Strategy, 2020*)

   (a) Analyse the factors that influence housing choices.
   Refer to:
   - socio-economic factors
   - availability of housing
   - national housing policy. (18)

   (b) Outline the conditions that are required in order to qualify for mortgage approval. (16)

   (c) Name and describe **one** type of mortgage available to house purchasers. (16)

5. **Marriage is still very popular in Ireland. In 2015, religious ceremonies accounted for the highest proportion of marriages (66.3%). Civil ceremonies were the most popular choice for non-religious marriage ceremonies (28%). In recent years the Humanist Association has also risen in popularity with 5.7% of marriages.** (*Central Statistics Office, 2016*)

   (a) Outline the variations that exist in marriages today. (16)

   (b) Discuss the benefits of pre-marriage courses for couples preparing for marriage. (16)

   (c) Evaluate **each** of the following options available to couples experiencing difficulties in their marriage:
   - marriage counselling
   - family mediation
   - legal separation. (18)

Section C

Answer **one elective question** from this section.
Candidates who submitted Textiles, Fashion and Design coursework for examination may **only** attempt **elective question 2**.

Elective 1 – Home Design and Management (80 marks)
Candidates selecting this elective must answer **1(a)** and either **1(b)** or **1(c)**.

1.(a) The Murphy family live in a bungalow with their two children, John (11 years) and Emily (4 years).

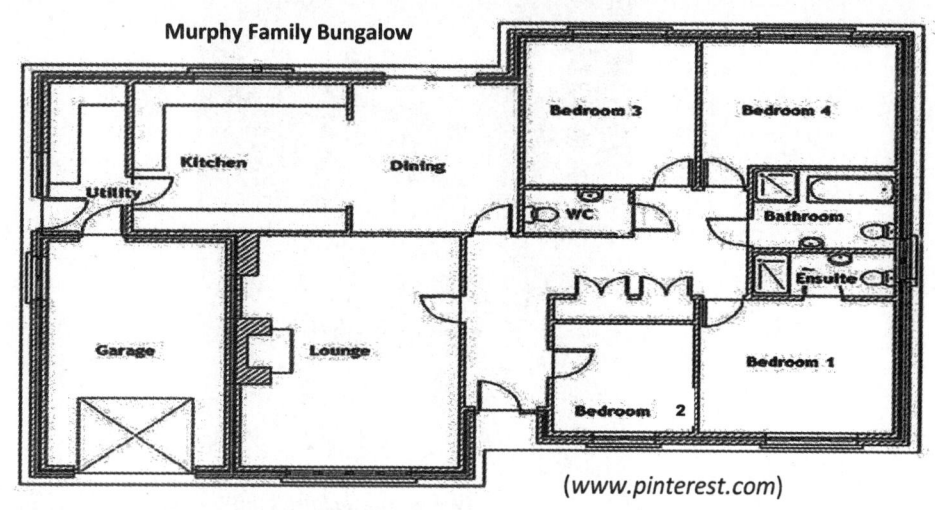

Murphy Family Bungalow

(*www.pinterest.com*)

- (i) Evaluate the suitability of the home for the family's present and future needs. Suggest modifications, if required. (20)

- (ii) Identify potential energy inefficiencies in a home **and** suggest strategies for improvement. (15)

- (iii) Write an informative note on the Building Energy Rating (BER) certificate. (15)

and

1.(b) **To the greatest extent possible, every household in Ireland will have access to secure, good quality housing suited to their needs at an affordable price and in a sustainable community.**
(*Vision Statement: Department of Housing, Planning, Community and Local Government*)

- (i) Evaluate the adequacy of social housing provision in Ireland. (18)

- (ii) Comment on the importance of **each** of the following services for new housing developments:
    - schools
    - transport
    - refuse collection. (12)

or

1.(c) **Proper ventilation is vital to a family's health and comfort.**

- (i) Outline the importance of adequate ventilation in the home. (12)

- (ii) Recommend **one** natural **and one** artificial method of ventilation suitable for a kitchen / living area. Explain the underlying principle of **each** method. (18)

Elective 2 – Textiles, Fashion and Design (40 marks)

Candidates selecting this elective must answer **2(a)** and either **2(b)** or **2(c)**.

2.(a) The athleisure trend is turning workout wear into a serious style statement.
People of every age are wearing workout clothes all day.

(*www.marieclaire.com*)

(i) Comment on the outfit shown in the picture above.
Refer to:
- comfort
- aesthetic appeal
- current fashion trend. (15)

(ii) Discuss the influence of trend setters **and** the media on fashion. (10)

and

2.(b) Blending is combining different fibres together to achieve a desired product characteristic.

Write a profile of **one** blended fabric.
Refer to:
- fibre production
- fabric properties
- uses. (15)

or

2.(c) The textile and fashion industry is one which is market-driven, with high levels of skill, imagination and creativity.

(i) Outline how the Irish fashion industry is promoted at home and abroad. (9)

(ii) Name and give details of **one** career opportunity in the textile and fashion industry. (6)

Elective 3 – Social Studies (80 marks)

Candidates selecting this elective must answer **3(a)** and either **3(b)** or **3(c)**.

3.(a) Unemployment in Ireland is now at its lowest level since December 2008. Total numbers unemployed have now fallen by 52% from the 327,000 peak recorded in 2011.

	2011	2012	2013	2014	2015	2016
Unemployment rates in Ireland	15.1%	14.1%	12.2%	10.2%	8.9%	7.2%

(The Irish Times, 2016)

(i) Comment on the information provided above and analyse why unemployment rates have changed in Ireland. (20)

(ii) Discuss the effects of unemployment on individuals, families **and** society. (20)

(iii) Name **and** give details of **one** scheme to reduce expenditure for low-income families. (10)

and

3.(b) The percentage of men exceeds the percentage of women in the labour force.

(i) Analyse the factors that influence the participation of women in employment. (15)

(ii) Comment and elaborate on the childcare options available for working parents. (15)

or

3.(c) The number of people emigrating remains high, despite improvements in the economy and a fall in unemployment.

(i) People often move from place to place in search of work, discuss the impact this has on individuals and their families. (20)

(ii) Outline how a person's work ethic influences their attitude to work. (10)

Write your Examination Number here

2016. M48

Coimisiún na Scrúduithe Stáit
State Examinations Commission

Leaving Certificate Examination, 2016

HOME ECONOMICS – SCIENTIFIC AND SOCIAL

HIGHER LEVEL

CENTRE STAMP

WEDNESDAY, 8 JUNE – AFTERNOON, 2.00 to 4.30

280/320 MARKS

Instructions to Candidates

Section A   There are **twelve** questions in this section.
Candidates are required to answer any **ten** questions.
Each question carries **6** marks.
Write your answers in the spaces provided on the examination paper.

Section B   There are **five** questions in this section.
Candidates are required to answer **Question 1** and any other two questions.
Question 1 is worth **80** marks.
Questions 2, 3, 4 and **5** are worth **50** marks each.
Write your answers in the separate answer book provided.

Section C   There are **three** questions in this section.
Candidates are required to answer **one** elective question to include
part (a) and either **part (b)** or **part (c)**.
Candidates who submitted Textiles, Fashion and Design coursework for examination may attempt only Question 2 from this section.
Electives **1** and **3** are worth **80** marks each. Elective **2** is worth **40** marks.
Write your answers in the separate answer book provided.

You must return your examination paper with your answer book at the end of the examination.

Section A

Answer any <u>ten</u> questions from this section.
Each question is worth 6 marks.
Write your answers in the spaces provided.

1. Name **one** food source of **each** of the proteins listed below. (6)

Proteins	Food source
Casein	
Actin	
Albumin	

2. State **one** function of *omega 3 fatty acids* in the diet. (6)

   _____

   _____

   Name **two** different food sources of *omega 3 fatty acids*.

   (i) _____ (ii) _____

3. Explain *food fortification*. (6)

   _____

   _____

   Name **one** fortified food / product and explain how it benefits the consumer.

   Fortified food / product _____

   Benefit _____

4. Give **three** functions of folic acid (folate). (6)

   (i) _____

   (ii) _____

   (iii) _____

5. State **two** advantages of including tofu in the diet. (6)

   (i) _____

   (ii) _____

   Other than tofu, name **two** protein alternatives that can be used in a vegan diet.

   (i) _____ (ii) _____

6. Write a note on **two** of the following: (6)

   Genetically modified food _____
   _____
   _____

   Organic food / produce _____
   _____
   _____

   Added-value food _____
   _____
   _____

7. Name the parts A, B and C as shown on the diagram of a yeast cell. (6)

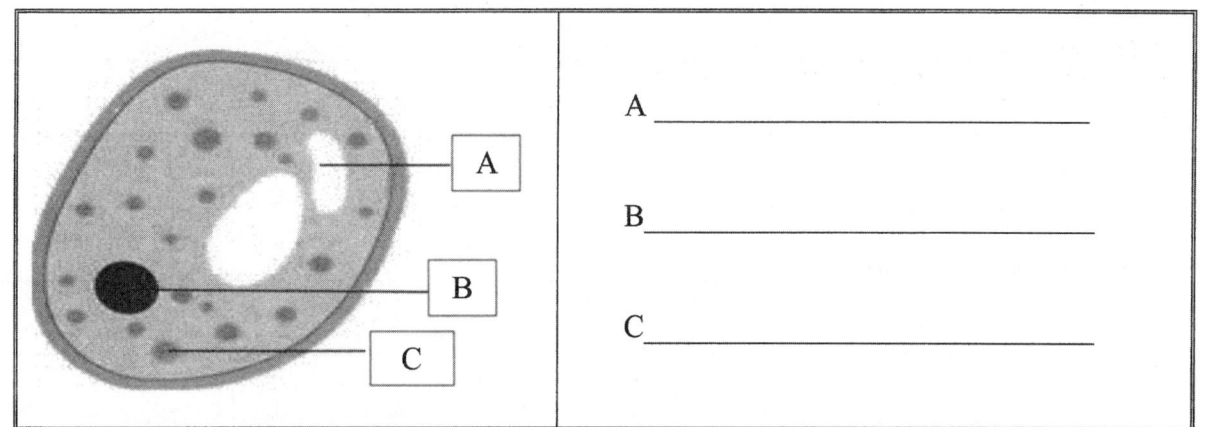

A _____

B _____

C _____

(www.bing.com/images)

8. In relation to the Hazard Analysis Critical Control Point (HACCP) system, explain **each** of the following terms. Give **one** example in each case. (6)

Hazard _____

_____

Example _____

Control measure _____

_____

Example _____

9. State the purpose of consumer research. (6)

_____

_____

Name and describe **one** method of consumer research.

_____

_____

10. Explain **each** of the following: (6)

    Life assurance _____

    _____

    _____

    Mortgage protection policy _____

    _____

    _____

11. List **two** desirable properties of fabric used in upholstered furniture. (6)

    (i) _____

    (ii) _____

    What information does the following label convey to the consumer?

    _____

    _____

    _____

    _____

12. Name **one** cause of air pollution and state the effect of this pollution on the environment. Explain how air pollution can be reduced. (6)

    Cause _____

    Effect _____

    _____

    Reduction measure _____

    _____

Section B

Answer Question 1 and any other two questions from this section.
Question 1 is worth 80 marks. Questions 2, 3, 4 and 5 are worth 50 marks each.

1. **Current intakes of dietary fibre are generally inadequate in adults, with over 80% not meeting the European Food Safety Authority (EFSA) recommendation of 25-30 grams per day.** *(National Adult Nutrition Survey, 2011)*

   The chart below provides information on the contribution of different foods to dietary fibre intake in Ireland for adults aged 18-64 years and those over 65 years.

	18 - 64 years		≥ 65 years	
Foods	%	grams	%	grams
Bread and rolls	26	4.8	29	5.4
Vegetables and vegetable dishes	17	3.3	18	3.2
Potatoes and potato products	13	2.2	12	2.0
Fruit and fruit juices	10	2.1	15	3.1
Breakfast cereals	9	2.0	10	2.1
Others	25	4.8	16	3.2
Total	100	19.2	100	19.0

   (a) Using the information provided in the chart, comment **and** elaborate on the contribution of **four** foods to the intake of dietary fibre with reference to the **two** categories of people identified above. (24)

   (b) Suggest **three** strategies to increase the intake of dietary fibre in order to meet the European Food Safety Authority (EFSA) recommendation. (12)

   (c) Evaluate the benefits of a diet rich in fibre. (15)

   (d) Name **and** give an account of **one** bowel disease.
   Refer to symptoms / effects. (9)

   (e) **Evening work, night shifts and rotating work schedules can have a negative effect on normal meal patterns.**

   Suggest how individuals who have an irregular work schedule can manage to achieve a healthy balanced lifestyle and good dietary practices. (20)

2. **Fish has long been recognised as one of nature's best foods and with its rich supply of nutrients it is one of the few foods that can truly be called a superfood.**

    (a) Discuss the nutritive value **and** the contribution of fresh fish / fish products to the diet. (20)

    (b) **Fish must be used or processed as soon as possible after being caught as spoilage occurs very quickly.**
Outline the main causes of fish spoilage. (15)

    (c) **Oily fish and fish liver oils can make a significant contribution to a persons' intake of vitamin D.**
Give an account of vitamin D and refer to:
- type / form
- properties
- effects of deficiency. (15)

3. **As more women enter the workforce and lifestyles change, global demand for frozen meals and ingredients will grow.** *(Bord Bia, 2013)*

    (a) Outline the benefits of incorporating frozen foods in meal planning. (12)

    (b) Set out details of **one** method of freezing fresh vegetables.
Refer to:
- description of the method used
- underlying principle involved
- the effect of freezing on the food. (20)

    (c) Evaluate the role of packaging / labelling in relation to **each** of the following:
- suitability for purpose
- environmental impact
- as a source of consumer information. (18)

4. 'While consumers are more optimistic about their financial outlook, they remain cautious, giving due consideration to all types of spend from grocery to big ticket items.'
   (Retail Ireland, September 2014)

   (a) Discuss how consumer shopping patterns have changed over the past 10 years **and** suggest reasons for such changes. (20)

   (b) Give details of **four** merchandising techniques used by retailers to maximise consumer spending. (20)

   (c) Name **and** give details of **one** statutory agency that protects consumers. (10)

5. **As the world's oldest form of human relationship, the family has survived thousands of years, adapting itself constantly to changing socio-economic conditions and the progress of humanity.**

   (a) Analyse the social **and** economic changes that affect contemporary families. (20)

   (b) Explain how the family can meet the physical **and** psychological needs of children so that they can contribute to and succeed in a rapidly changing society. (18)

   (c) Discuss the challenges that may be experienced by the parents of a child with special needs. (12)

Section C

Answer **one** elective question from this section.
Candidates who submitted Textiles, Fashion and Design coursework
for examination may attempt **only** Question 2.

Elective 1 – Home Design and Management (80 marks)
Candidates selecting this elective must answer 1(a) and either 1(b) **or** 1(c).

1.(a) The idea of your own self-build house construction can be a very compelling idea to give you a bespoke dream home tailored to your lifestyle and requirements.

   (i) Discuss the factors that influence a family's choice of location **and** house style when building a house. (24)

   (ii) Outline the procedures involved in obtaining full planning permission. (14)

   (iii) Give an account of the specific housing requirements of the following groups:
   - people with disabilities
   - homeless people. (12)

and

1.(b) A variety of technologies are available for heating houses.

   (i) Discuss the options available when choosing a heating system for a new house. (12)

   (ii) Describe **one** type of central heating system suitable for a family home.
   Refer to:
   - type of heating system
   - underlying principle
   - devices used to control thermal comfort in the home. (18)

or

1.(c) Home office spaces have become very popular as many people now run a business from home.

   (i) In relation to lighting:
   - outline the principles that should be considered when planning a lighting system for a home office / study
   - name and describe **one** type of lighting suitable for the space. (14)

   (ii) Give **four** guidelines to be considered when choosing furniture to create a functional **and** aesthetic office space. (16)

Elective 2 – Textiles, Fashion and Design (40 marks)
Candidates selecting this elective must answer 2(a) and either 2(b) or 2(c).

2.(a) **Fashion trends have evolved through the ages, some have recurred, others have discontinued but all have contributed to fashion today.**

    (i) Critically evaluate male **or** female fashion trends of the past decade. (9)

    (ii) Sketch and design an outfit that incorporates **one** current fashion trend. (9)

    (iii) In relation to the outfit, give details of:
- the fashion trend
- suitability for purpose. (7)

and

2.(b) **Fibres are the basis of all textiles.**

    (i) Differentiate between regenerated fibres **and** synthetic fibres and give **one** example of each. (6)

    (ii) Name and describe **each** of the following:
- **one** method of colour application to fabric
- **one** method of design application to fabric. (9)

or

2.(c) **'Fashion fades, only style remains the same.'** *(Coco Chanel)*

    (i) Discuss the work of **one** milliner **or** fashion designer. (9)

    (ii) Evaluate the growing popularity of accessories in completing an outfit. (6)

Elective 3 – Social Studies (80 marks)
Candidates selecting this elective must answer 3(a) and either 3(b) or 3(c).

3.(a) **There are 755,570 people living in poverty in Ireland. This is a rise of 55,000 since 2011, over 23,000 of these are children.** *(Social Justice Ireland, November 2015)*

    (i) Define *poverty*. (8)

    (ii) In relation to poverty explain **each** of the following:
- relative poverty
- the poverty line
- the cycle of poverty. (12)

    (iii) Discuss the social **and** economic reasons why poverty continues to exist in today's society. (20)

    (iv) Name and give details of **one** voluntary organisation which works to alleviate poverty in Ireland. (10)

and

3.(b) **Education has a direct effect on the overall development of the child and on the adult they will become.**

    (i) Discuss the role of education in the social, emotional **and** intellectual development of children in their formative years. (18)

    (ii) Name and give details of **one** statutory education initiative provided for pre-school children. (12)

or

3.(c) **Gender roles are defined by the socio-cultural norms of any society.**

    (i) Describe how gender roles have changed within the contemporary family **and** outline the effect on family members. (15)

    (ii) Discuss the impact of dual earner families on family life with reference to:
- role overload
- role conflict. (15)

Write your Examination Number here   2015. M48

Coimisiún na Scrúduithe Stáit
State Examinations Commission

Leaving Certificate Examination, 2015

HOME ECONOMICS – SCIENTIFIC AND SOCIAL

HIGHER LEVEL

CENTRE STAMP

WEDNESDAY, 3 JUNE – AFTERNOON, 2.00 to 4.30

280/320 MARKS

Instructions to Candidates

Section A There are **twelve** questions in this section.
Candidates are required to answer any **ten** questions.
Each question carries **6** marks.
Write your answers in the spaces provided on the examination paper.

Section B There are **five** questions in this section.
Candidates are required to answer **Question 1 and any other two questions**.
Question 1 is worth **80** marks.
Questions 2, 3, 4 and **5** are worth **50** marks each.
Write your answers in the separate answer book provided.

Section C There are **three** questions in this section.
Candidates are required to answer **one** elective question to include **part (a)** and either **part (b)** or **part (c)**.
Candidates who submitted Textiles, Fashion and Design coursework for examination may attempt only Question 2 from this section.
Electives **1** and **3** are worth **80** marks each. Elective **2** is worth **40** marks.
Write your answers in the separate answer book provided.

You must return your examination paper with your answer book at the end of the examination.

Section A

Answer any ten questions from this section.
Each question is worth 6 marks.
Write your answers in the spaces provided.

1. Explain protein deamination. (6)

   _____

   _____

   _____

2. Complete the table below in relation to carbohydrates. (6)

Class	Example	Food source
Monosaccharides		
Disaccharides		
Polysaccharides		

3. Enumerate **three** biological functions of water. (6)

   (i) _____

   (ii) _____

   (iii) _____

4. In relation to lipids explain **each** of the following: (6)

   Smoke point _____

   _____

   Flash point _____

   _____

5. State the nutritional significance of **each** of the following parts of the wheat grain. (6)

	Nutritional significance
Bran	
Endosperm	
Germ	

6. Outline **three** conditions necessary to ensure accurate results when carrying out sensory analysis tests. (6)

(i) _____

(ii) _____

(iii) _____

7. Classify sauces and give **one** example in each class. (6)

Classification	**Example / Sauce**

8. Explain how **two** of the following assist in the control of enzymic food spoilage. (6)

Blanching	
Cold temperatures	
Acids	

175

9. State the purpose of family resource management. **(6)**

_____

_____

_____

List the **three** components of management.

(i) _____

(ii) _____

(iii) _____

10. State **one** advantage and **one** disadvantage of using credit to pay household utility bills. **(6)**

Advantage _____

_____

_____

Disadvantage _____

_____

_____

11. State the function of **each** of the following parts of the refrigerator: **(6)**

Thermostat _____

_____

Refrigerant _____

_____

12. Outline **two** functions of the Citizens Information Board. (6)

(i) _____

_____

(ii) _____

_____

Section B

**Answer Question 1 and any other two questions from this section.
Question 1 is worth 80 marks. Questions 2, 3, 4 and 5 are worth 50 marks each.**

1.
> *A survey was conducted to identify the level and type of marketing of foodstuffs in post primary schools in the Republic of Ireland.*
>
> *An extract from the summary of the main findings showed that a variety of food outlets e.g. tuck shops (53.2%), canteens (53.2%) and drinks vending machines (44.7%) are in operation in post-primary schools in Ireland, with a high proportion of schools also reporting a shop close to the grounds (64.4%).*
>
> *A variety of healthy foods are available through one or more of these outlets including water (92.1%), juice (78.4%), sandwiches (73.9%) and fruit (62%). However, confectionery (74.1%), salty snacks/crisps (57.2%), fizzy/high sugar drinks (51.8%), diet drinks (50.2%) and biscuits, cakes and pastries (32.6%) are also widely available.*

(a) Using the information given above, comment and elaborate on (i) the provision **and** (ii) the nutritional significance of the foods and beverages available to students in post primary schools. **(24)**

(b) Poor food choices have contributed to 42% of teenage girls and 23% of teenage boys not getting enough calcium in their diet.

Give an account of *calcium* and include reference to:
- sources
- biological functions
- factors assisting/inhibiting absorption. **(18)**

(c) Explain (i) what is osteoporosis;

(ii) the main factors that increase the risk of developing osteoporosis. **(18)**

(d) Discuss the role of parents in shaping their children's food choices. **(20)**

2. **Over 85% of adults in Ireland enjoy eggs at least once a week, with 56% of men and 47% of women eating eggs two to three times per week.** *(Bord Bia, 2014)*

    (a) Set out the results of a study you have carried out on eggs.
Refer to:

- nutritional significance
- contribution to the diet
- properties and related culinary uses. (40)

    (b) Explain how quality is assured in egg production in order to minimise food safety risks. (10)

3. **Micro-organisms are commonly used in the production of many foods.**

    (a) Discuss **four** conditions necessary for the growth of moulds. (16)

    (b) Write a detailed account of **one** type of mould with reference to the following:

- name
- description/characteristics
- reproduction. (22)

    (c) Outline the uses of micro-organisms in food production. (12)

4. **Money management skills are vital to running the house as a financial unit.**

   (a) Analyse **three** social factors that affect household income. (18)

   (b) Design a family budget (two adults and two young children) where the net weekly income is €650. Give a reason for the proposed allocation of income for each area of expenditure. (18)

   (c) Recommend **one** type of savings scheme suitable for a family.
   Refer to:
   - name of institution
   - type of savings scheme
   - interest paid
   - ease of access to funds
   - tax payable. (14)

5. **Each year thousands of couples get married in Ireland. The majority of these marriages begin with some form of official ceremony with Church ceremonies being the most popular.** (*Accord*)

   (a) (i) Define marriage as it exists in Irish law.

   (ii) Set out the legal requirements for marriage in Ireland. (21)

   (b) Discuss the rights **and** responsibilities of partners within a marriage relationship. (20)

   (c) Outline the conditions required for granting a divorce under the Family Law (Divorce) Act, 1996. (9)

Section C

Answer one elective question from this section.
Candidates who submitted Textiles, Fashion and Design coursework
for examination may attempt **only** Question 2.

Elective 1 – Home Design and Management (80 marks)
Candidates selecting this elective must answer 1(a) and either 1(b) **or** 1(c).

1.(a) Today the kitchen is the new living room, a modern hybrid of a living room, kitchen and dining area.

   (i) Discuss the factors that influence the interior design of a contemporary style kitchen/living area for a family with a member who has special needs.
   Refer to **each** of the following:
   - ergonomics
   - aesthetic and comfort factors. **(18)**

   (ii) Differentiate between thermoplastic **and** thermosetting plastics.
   Refer to:
   - properties
   - examples
   - uses. **(20)**

   (iii) Outline the effects of condensation in the home **and** state how condensation may be reduced/prevented. **(12)**

and

1.(b) (i) Name and explain **three** charges shown on a domestic electricity bill. **(12)**

   (ii) Explain how **each** of the following impact on electrical safety:
   - fuses
   - miniature circuit breakers (MCBs)
   - earth wire. **(18)**

or

1.(c) **Fresh water is a finite and vulnerable resource, essential to sustain life, development and the environment.** *(Global Water Partnership)*

   (i) Describe the cold water system in a house. **(15)**

   (ii) Write an informative note on water with reference to **each** of the following:
   - sources of domestic water in rural **or** urban areas
   - water quality
   - water charges. **(15)**

Elective 2 – Textiles, Fashion and Design (40 marks)
Candidates selecting this elective must answer 2(a) and either 2(b) or 2(c).

2.(a) Playsuits and jumpsuits have evolved from men's clothing to chic and versatile garments and are important fashion staples in every person's wardrobe.

(i) Sketch **and** describe a playsuit/jumpsuit you would choose to wear for an occasion of your choice. (9)

(ii) You plan to make the garment. Give details of **each** of the following:
- body measurements required
- type of fabric you would select and reason for choice
- outline plan of work to assemble the garment. (16)

and

2.(b) Write a profile of **one** fabric manufactured from natural fibres.
Refer to:
- fibre production
- fabric properties
- uses. (15)

or

2.(c) As a practice of expression and as a way to individualism it is obvious that music and fashion are closely linked.

(i) Discuss, giving examples, how music and/or musicians have influenced trends in fashion over the years. (6)

(ii) Give examples of how a garment can be restyled to reflect a modern trend. (9)

Elective 3 – Social Studies (80 marks)
Candidates selecting this elective must answer 3(a) and either 3(b) or 3(c).

3.(a) **While the improvement in the Irish economy is creating more opportunities for people to find work, there remains significant challenges in terms of youth and long-term unemployment.** *(The Irish Times, November 2014)*

    (i) Discuss how changes in the availability of work have affected individuals and families in Ireland. **(20)**

    (ii) Discuss, giving examples, how flexibility in working hours has impacted on work/life balance for many people. **(20)**

    (iii) Name **and** give details of **one** statutory initiative aimed at creating employment. **(10)**

and

3.(b)   (i) Evaluate **three** supports that are available to improve the accessibility of second-level education for all students. **(15)**

    (ii) Explain, giving examples, how education prepares students for participation in employment. **(15)**

or

3.(c) **Although an individual's leisure can often be affected by numerous external factors such as age, race, income and gender, there is no denying the benefits of incorporating a small amount of leisure into a person's routine.**

    (i) Discuss, giving examples, the role of leisure activities in personal development. Refer to the following factors:
- physical
- social
- emotional. **(18)**

    (ii) Name **and** evaluate **two** leisure facilities popular with retired people. **(12)**

2024.M47

Coimisiún na Scrúduithe Stáit
State Examinations Commission

Leaving Certificate Examination 2024

Home Economics - Scientific and Social

Section A and Answerbook

Ordinary Level

Wednesday 5 June   Afternoon 2:00 - 4:30

280 or 320 marks

Examination Number

Date of Birth

For example, 3rd February 2005 is entered as 03 02 05

Centre Stamp

Instructions

Write your Examination Number and your Date of Birth in the boxes on the front cover.

Write your answers to all parts of the examination into this answerbook. This answerbook will be scanned and your work will be presented to an examiner on screen. Anything that you write outside of the answer areas may not be seen by the examiner.

Write your answers in blue or black pen. You may use pencil for sketches, graphs and diagrams only.

There are three sections to this examination. Questions for **Sections B and C** are supplied separately but your answers must be written in this answerbook.

Section A   60 marks
Answer any **ten** questions in this section.
Each question carries 6 marks.

Section B   180 marks
Answer **Question 1** and any other **two** questions from this section.
Question 1 is worth 80 marks.
Questions 2, 3, 4 and 5 are worth 50 marks each.

Section C   40 or 80 marks
Answer **one** elective question **or** Question 4 (core) to include **part (a)** and either **part (b) or part (c)**.

If you submitted *Textiles, Fashion and Design* coursework for examination, you may only attempt Question 2 from this section.

Electives 1 and 3 are worth 80 marks each.
Elective 2 is worth 40 marks.
Question 4 (core) is worth 80 marks.

Leaving Certificate Examination 2024
Home Economics – Ordinary level
Section A and answerbook

Section A   60 marks

Answer any **ten** questions from this section.
Each question carries 6 marks.
Write your answers in the spaces provided.

1. Indicate with a tick (✓) whether **each** of the following statements is true or false.

	True	False
Meat contains fibres and connective tissue		
1 g of protein provides 4 kilocalories of energy to the body		
Eggs are a low biological value food		

2. State **two** functions of Vitamin C in the body.

   (i) _____

   (ii) _____

   Name **one** dietary source of Vitamin C.

   _____

3. Using the terms listed below, complete the following statements in relation to energy.

   empty kilocalories   **energy balance**   **obesity**

   Over indulgence in sugar-based foods can cause _____.

   _____ are calories that have little nutritional value.

   Energy input equals energy output is known as _____.

Leaving Certificate Examination 2024
Home Economics – Ordinary level
Section A and answerbook

4. Outline **two** factors that affect the tenderness of meat.

(i)
(ii)

List **two** ways of tenderising meat.

(i)
(ii)

5. Indicate with a tick (✓) whether **each** of the following statements is true or false.

	True	False
The bran layer of cereals is high in fibre		
Heat causes starch grains to swell and burst		
A roux sauce contains different amounts of fat and flour		

6. Outline **three** lifestyle changes recommended for an obese person trying to lose weight.

(i)
(ii)
(iii)

7. Name **two** types of pastry and name a different dish that can be made from each type.

Type of pastry	Dish

8. Outline **three** guidelines to follow when freezing fresh food.

(i)
(ii)
(iii)

9. Match the following methods of heat transfer with the correct definition.

Conduction   Convection   Radiation

Definition	Method of heat transfer
Heat travels in straight lines and heats/cooks the first solid object it touches	
Heat travels through a liquid or gas, causing it to rise, cold liquid or gas moves in to take its place	
Heat travels through the molecules of a solid object until it is fully heated	

10. Outline **three** consumer rights when buying goods.

(i)
(ii)
(iii)

11. State **three** advantages of teenagers becoming regular savers.

(i)
(ii)
(iii)

12. Explain how the following criteria influence the consumer when selecting textiles for the household.

Suitability for purpose
Personal choice
Cost

13. In relation to insurance, state **two** benefits of life assurance.

(i)
(ii)

14. Describe three guidelines to follow when using a microwave oven.

(i)
(ii)
(iii)

Answerbook for Sections B and C

Instructions

Questions for **Sections B** and **Section C** are supplied separately.

Start each question on a new page. Write the question number in the box at the top of each page. Use the left-hand column to label each part, as shown below.

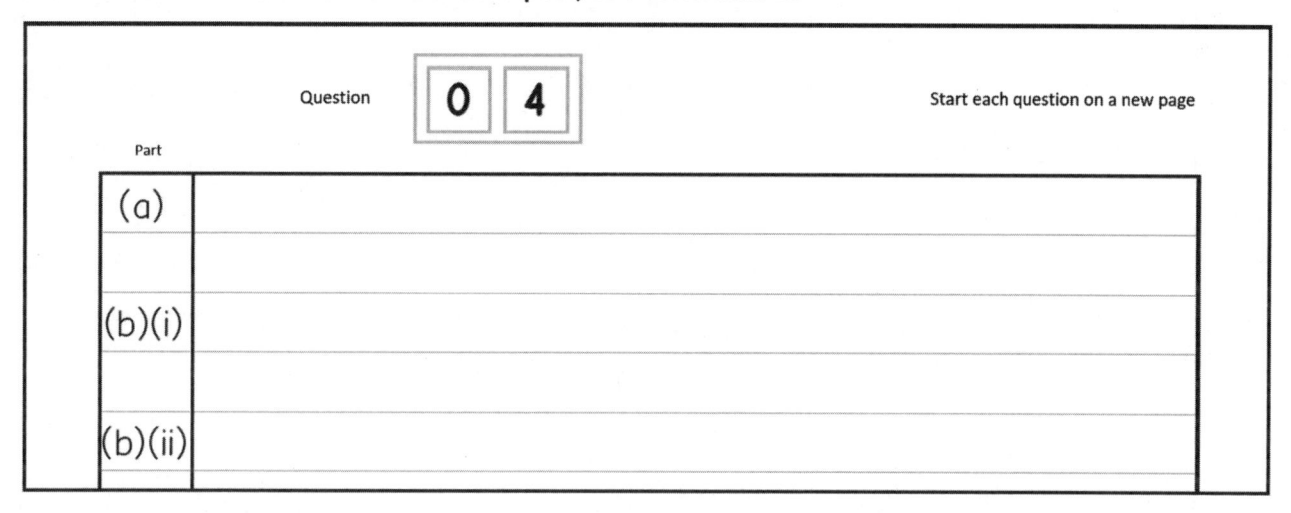

Part	Question 0 4 — Start each question on a new page
(a)	
(b)(i)	
(b)(ii)	

You do not need to use all of the pages in this answerbook. If you run out of space in this answerbook, you may ask the superintendent for more paper.

Write your answers in blue or black pen. You may use pencil for sketches, graphs and diagrams only.

---

*New Format: From 2020 the returnable answerbook is provided with this section of the Exam Paper

---

Leaving Certificate Examination 2024
Home Economics – Ordinary level
Section A and answerbook

Do not write on this page

Copyright notice
This examination paper may contain text or images for which the State Examinations Commission is not the copyright owner, and which may have been adapted, for the purpose of assessment, without the authors' prior consent. This examination paper has been prepared in accordance with Section 53(5) of the *Copyright and Related Rights Act, 2000*. Any subsequent use for a purpose other than the intended purpose is not authorised. The Commission does not accept liability for any infringement of third-party rights arising from unauthorised distribution or use of this examination paper.

Leaving Certificate – Ordinary Level

Home Economics - Scientific and Social
Section A and Answerbook

Wednesday 5 June
Afternoon 2:00 - 4:30

2024. M47

2024L098G2EL

Coimisiún na Scrúduithe Stáit
State Examinations Commission

LEAVING CERTIFICATE EXAMINATION 2024

Home Economics – Scientific and Social

ORDINARY LEVEL

Section B and Section C

WEDNESDAY 5 JUNE   AFTERNOON 2:00 – 4:30

Section B   180 marks
Answer **Question 1** and any other **two** questions from this section.
Question 1 is worth 80 marks.
Questions 2, 3, 4 and 5 are worth 50 marks each.

Section C   40 or 80 marks
Answer **one** elective question **or** Question 4 (core), to include **part (a)** and either **part (b) or part (c)**.

If you submitted *Textiles, Fashion and Design* coursework for examination, you may only attempt Question 2 from this section.

Electives 1 and 3 are worth 80 marks each.
Elective 2 is worth 40 marks.
Question 4 (core) is worth 80 marks.

Do not hand this up.
This document will not be returned to the
State Examinations Commission.

Section B   **180 marks**

Answer **Question 1** and any other **two** questions from this section.
Question 1 is worth 80 marks. Questions 2, 3, 4 and 5 are worth 50 marks each.
Write your answers in the answerbook containing **Section A**.

Question 1

'All around the world, people choose to eat different food for many different reasons.'
(*www.foodfactoflife.org.uk*)

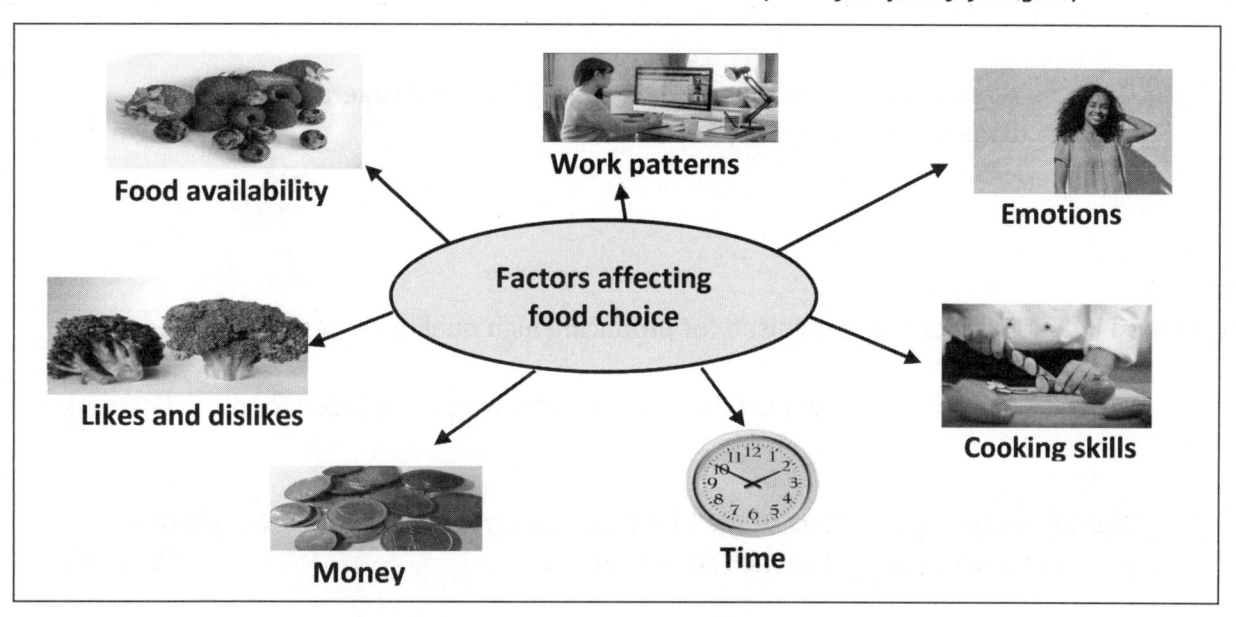

[Diagram: Factors affecting food choice — Food availability, Work patterns, Emotions, Cooking skills, Time, Money, Likes and dislikes]

(a) Using the information presented in the table, discuss **five** factors that affect a person's food choices.   (20 marks)

(b) Give an account of carbohydrates under **each** of the following headings:
- classification
- functions in the body
- dietary sources.   (28 marks)

(c) Outline **three** different ways a person can increase the amount of fibre in their diet.   (12 marks)

(d) Describe **four** ways consumers can reduce food waste when planning meals and purchasing foods.   (20 marks)

Question 2
'Approximately 8% of Irish people are following a vegetarian based diet.' *(Bord Bia, 2021)*

(a) Give an account of **(i)** the nutritive value **and (ii)** dietetic value of fruit and vegetables.
(20 marks)

(b) Having regard to current healthy eating guidelines, set out a menu (3 meals) for one day for a vegetarian to ensure their nutritional needs are met. (18 marks)

(c) Describe **three** guidelines to follow when storing fruit and vegetables in order to maintain their quality. (12 marks)

Question 3
Ireland's food industry is globally recognised for producing high quality processed foods.

(a) Describe **four** food additives used in the manufacture of processed foods. (20 marks)

(b) Identify **three** major sectors of the Irish food industry **and** give **one** example of a food product produced in **each** sector named. (15 marks)

(c) Evaluate the role of packaging in relation to **each** of the following:
- suitability for purpose
- environmental impact
- as a source of consumer information. (15 marks)

Leaving Certificate Examination 2024
Home Economics – Ordinary level
Sections B and C

Question 4
'From time to time problems will arise with goods and services.' (www.ccpc.ie)

(a) Describe **four** factors that influence consumers when selecting goods and services. (20 marks)

(b) Give an account of the Small Claims Court procedure used to resolve a consumer dispute over goods or services. (20 marks)

(c) Explain how the Sale of Goods and Supply Services Act 1980, protects the consumer. (10 marks)

Question 5
'Caring for our family members has always been a fundamental part of ethical living.'

© President Michael D. Higgins

(a) Describe each of the following functions of the family:
- physical
- emotional
- social
- economic. (20 marks)

(b) Explain how the state assists the family in carrying out their physical, social and economic functions. (15 marks)

(c) Discuss **three** advantages of a positive parent-child relationship within the family. (15 marks)

Leaving Certificate Examination 2024
Home Economics – Ordinary level
Sections B and C

Section C   40 or 80 marks

Answer **one** elective question **or** Question 4 (core) to include **part (a)** and either **part (b) or (c)**.
If you submitted *Textiles, Fashion and Design* coursework for examination,
you may only attempt Question 2 from this section.
Write your answer in the answerbook containing **Section A**.

Elective 1 – Home Design and Management – 80 marks

Candidates selecting this elective must answer **1(a)** and either **1(b) or 1(c)**.

1.(a) 'The quality of drinking water is a powerful environmental determinant of health.'
(*www.hse.ie*)

(i) Describe **four** stages involved in the treatment of the public water supply to make it safe for people to drink. (20 marks)

(ii) Explain what precautions should be taken to prevent the cold-water supply freezing in the home during cold weather. (15 marks)

(iii) Describe the function of the following in relation to the cold-water supply of a house:
- service pipe
- ball valve
- storage tank. (15 marks)

and

1.(b) 'Over the past ten years the way we design our homes has changed a lot.' (*www.houzz.ie*)

(i) Describe the procedure to follow when applying for full planning permission to build a house. (15 marks)

(ii) Discuss the role of the following professional services when designing and building a house:
- architect
- engineer
- solicitor. (15 marks)

or

1.(c) All homes in Ireland should have good ventilation.

(i) Discuss **three** advantages of having good ventilation in the home. (15 marks)

(ii) Name **one** method of ventilation suitable for a kitchen **and** explain the underlying principle of the method named. (15 marks)

Elective 2 – Textiles, Fashion and Design – 40 marks

Candidates selecting this elective must answer **2(a)** and either **2(b) or 2(c)**.

2.(a) Sportwear needs to be practical but can also be stylish.

(www.pinterest.com)

- **(i)** Comment on the suitability of the sportswear outfits shown above.
  Refer to:
    - comfort
    - function
    - aesthetic appeal. (18 marks)

- **(ii)** Describe how emphasis as a design principle is applied to the outfits pictured above.
  (7 marks)

and

2.(b) 'Textiles have such an important bearing on our daily lives.' (www.coats.com)

Write a profile of a natural fibre under **each** of the following headings:
- fibre production
- properties
- test to identify a natural fibre. (15 marks)

or

2.(c) 'Fashion has two purposes comfort and love.' (*Coco Chanel*)

- **(i)** Describe **two** fashion trends currently popular in summer clothing. (6 marks)

- **(ii)** Discuss **three** factors that influence a person's choice when choosing work wear clothing. (9 marks)

Elective 3 – Social Studies – 80 marks

Candidates selecting this elective must answer **3(a)** and either **3(b)** or **3(c)**.

3.(a) 'Of women over 15 years of age in Ireland, more than 50% of them are in the workforce.'
(*www.cso.ie*)

    (i) Explain the following types of work:
- paid work
- unpaid work
- voluntary work. (15 marks)

    (ii) Discuss **three** reasons for the increased participation of women in the work force. (15 marks)

    (iii) Evaluate the impact of dual-earner families on family life. (20 marks)

and

3.(b) Leisure time is time that a person is free from work or other duties.

    (i) Discuss how family leisure activities are influenced by each of the following:
- gender
- age
- cultural influences. (15 marks)

    (ii) Evaluate the benefits of participating in leisure activities for family members. (15 marks)

or

3.(c) Social and economic changes have impacted on family life in Ireland today.

    (i) Evaluate the impact of the following on family life:
- improvements in the provision of education
- parenting roles within the family
- improved conditions at work. (15 marks)

    (ii) Describe how second-level education prepares students for participation in the workplace. (15 marks)

Leaving Certificate Examination 2024
Home Economics – Ordinary level
Sections B and C

Question 4 – Core – 80 marks

Candidates selecting this question must answer **4(a)** and either **4(b)** or **4(c)**.

4.(a) 'Your body needs lots of different nutrients to stay healthy.' (*www.safefood.net*)

  (i) Give an account of **(i)** the nutritive value **and (ii)** the dietetic value of milk. (20 marks)

  (ii) Describe **one** heat treatment used by manufacturers to extend the shelf life of milk. Refer to:
  - name of process
  - how the process is carried out
  - labelling. (18 marks)

  (iii) Outline **three** different ways that dairy foods can be included as part of a healthy diet. (12 marks)

and

4.(b) 'Choosing an electrical appliance, less is usually best.' (*www.electricireland.com*)

  (i) Discuss **three** factors that should be considered when choosing a kitchen appliance. (15 marks)

  (ii) Describe **three** guidelines to follow for the safe use of electrical kitchen appliances. (15 marks)

or

4.(c) 'There was a total of 23,173 marriages celebrated in Ireland in 2022.' (*www.cso.ie*)

  (i) Outline the conditions necessary for a marriage to be legally valid in Ireland. (15 marks)

  (ii) Discuss **three** responsibilities of a couple within a marriage relationship. (15 marks)

Leaving Certificate Examination 2024
Home Economics – Ordinary level
Sections B and C

Do not hand this up.

This document will not be returned to the State Examinations Commission

Copyright notice
This examination paper may contain text or images for which the State Examinations Commission is not the copyright owner, and which may have been adapted, for the purpose of assessment, without the authors' prior consent. This examination paper has been prepared in accordance with Section 53(5) of the Copyright and Related Rights Act, 2000. Any subsequent use for a purpose other than the intended purpose is not authorised. The Commission does not accept liability for any infringement of third-party rights arising from unauthorised distribution or use of this examination paper.

Leaving Certificate – Ordinary Level

Home Economics - Scientific and Social
Section B and Section C

Wednesday 5 June
Afternoon 2:00 – 4:30

2023.M47

Coimisiún na Scrúduithe Stáit
State Examinations Commission

Leaving Certificate Examination 2023

Home Economics - Scientific and Social

Section A and Answerbook

Ordinary Level

Wednesday 7 June   Afternoon 2:00 - 4:30

280 or 320 marks

Examination Number

Day and Month of Birth

For example, 3rd February is entered as 0302

Centre Stamp

Instructions

Write your Examination Number and your Day and Month of Birth in the boxes on the front cover.

Write your answers to all parts of the examination into this answerbook. This answerbook will be scanned and your work will be presented to an examiner on screen. Anything that you write outside of the answer areas may not be seen by the examiner.

Write your answers in blue or black pen. You may use pencil for sketches, graphs and diagrams only.

There are three sections in this examination. Questions for **Sections B and C** are supplied separately but your answers must be written in this answerbook.

Section A 60 marks
Answer **ten** questions in this section.
Each question carries 6 marks.

Section B 180 marks
Answer **Question 1** and any other **two** questions from this section.
Question 1 is worth 80 marks.
Questions 2, 3, 4 and 5 are worth 50 marks each.

Section C 40 or 80 marks
Answer **one** elective question **or** Question 4 (core) to include **part (a)** and either **part (b) or part (c)**.

If you submitted *Textiles, Fashion and Design* coursework for examination, you may only attempt Question 2 from this section.

Electives 1 and 3 are worth 80 marks each.
Elective 2 is worth 40 marks.
Question 4 (core) is worth 80 marks.

Section A

60 marks

Answer any **ten** questions from this section.
Each question carries 6 marks.
Write your answers in the spaces provided.

1. Indicate with a tick (✓) whether **each** of the following statements is true or false.

	True	False
Polyunsaturated fatty acids are present in oily fish		
Lipids (fats) contain the element nitrogen		
Adipose tissue protects delicate organs in the body		

2. List **three** factors that influence the energy requirements of adults.

(i)
(ii)
(iii)

3. Use the words below to complete the following statements in relation to protein.

        albumin   **coagulate**   **aeration**

When eggs are heated, protein chains _____.

_____ occurs when egg whites are whisked.

_____ is a protein present in the white of an egg.

205

4. State **two** functions of iron in the body.

(i)
(ii)

Name **one** dietary source of iron.

5. Indicate with a tick (✓) whether **each** of the following statements is true or false.

	True	False
Carbohydrate is converted into glucose during digestion		
Bile is produced in the stomach		
Enzymes are proteins essential for digestion		

6. In relation to cereals, name **one** different food product made from each of the following:

Cereal	Food product
Wheat	
Rice	
Maize/Corn	

7. Outline **three** different ways a teenager can increase the amount of fibre in their diet.

(i)
(ii)
(iii)

8. Name **one** different raising agent suitable for each of the following baked products.

Baked products	Raising agent
Sponge cake	
Bread	
Lemon drizzle cake	

9. Outline **three** guidelines to follow when using grilling as a method of cooking.

(i)
(ii)
(iii)

10. Indicate with a tick (✓) whether **each** of the following statements is true or false.

	True	False
Supplementary welfare allowance is means tested		
Child benefit is a universal welfare payment		
Working family payment is available to employees on low pay with children		

11. Name **one** type of credit available to consumers.

Outline **two** disadvantages of the type of credit named.

(i)

(ii)

12. Describe **three** functions of textiles in the home.

(i)

(ii)

(iii)

13. Outline **three** guidelines to follow when selecting a microwave oven.

(i)
(ii)
(iii)

14. What information does **each** of the following fabric care symbols convey to the consumer?

(www.beezzly.com)

(www.reddit.com)

Answerbook for Sections B and C

Instructions

Questions for **Sections B** and **C** are supplied separately.

Start each question on a new page. Write the question number in the box at the top of each page. Use the left-hand column to label each part, as shown below.

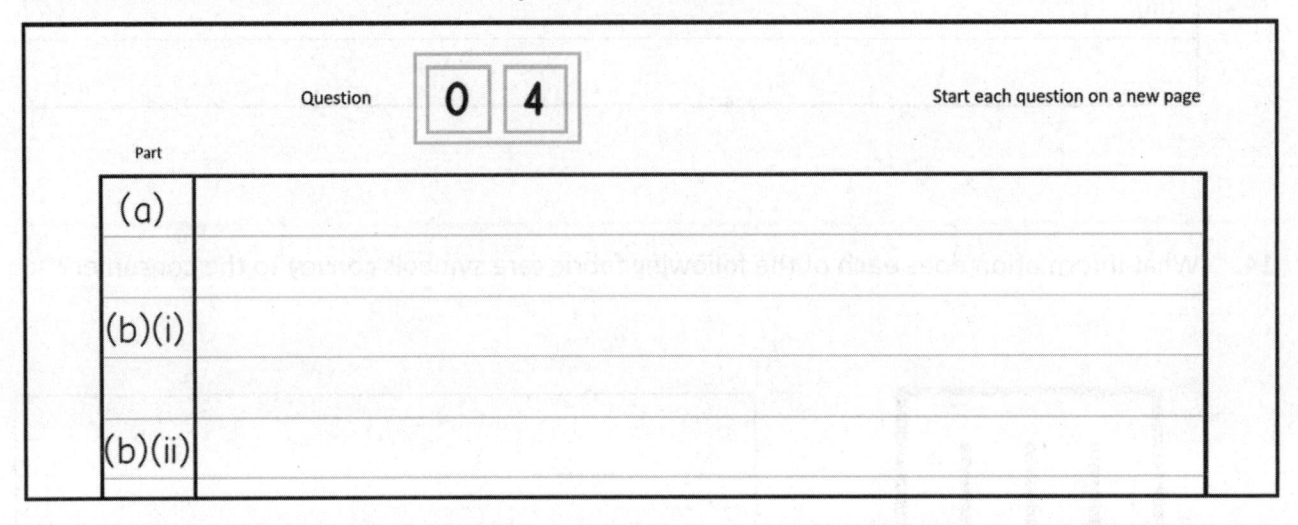

Part	Question 0 4 Start each question on a new page
(a)	
(b)(i)	
(b)(ii)	

You do not need to use all of the pages in this answerbook. If you run out of space in this answerbook, you may ask the superintendent for more paper.

Write your answers in blue or black pen. You may use pencil for sketches, graphs and diagrams only.

*New Format: From 2020 the returnable answerbook is provided with this section of the Exam Paper

Do not write on this page

Copyright notice
This examination paper may contain text or images for which the State Examinations Commission is not the copyright owner, and which may have been adapted, for the purpose of assessment, without the authors' prior consent. This examination paper has been prepared in accordance with *Section 53(5) of the Copyright and Related Rights Act, 2000*. Any subsequent use for a purpose other than the intended purpose is not authorised. The Commission does not accept liability for any infringement of third-party rights arising from unauthorised distribution or use of this examination paper.

Leaving Certificate – Ordinary Level

Home Economics - Scientific and Social Section A and Answerbook

Wednesday 7 June
Afternoon 2:00 - 4:30

2023.M47

2023L098G2EL

Coimisiún na Scrúduithe Stáit
State Examinations Commission

LEAVING CERTIFICATE EXAMINATION 2023

Home Economics – Scientific and Social

ORDINARY LEVEL
Section B and Section C

WEDNESDAY 7 JUNE   AFTERNOON 2:00 – 4:30

Section B 180 marks
Answer **Question 1** and any other **two** questions from this section.
Question 1 is worth 80 marks.
Questions 2, 3, 4 and 5 are worth 50 marks each.

Section C 40 or 80 marks
Answer **one** elective question **or** Question 4 (core) to include **part (a)** and either **part (b) or part (c)**.

If you submitted *Textiles, Fashion and Design* coursework for examination, you may only attempt Question 2 from this section.

Electives 1 and 3 are worth 80 marks each.
Elective 2 is worth 40 marks.
Question 4 (core) is worth 80 marks.

Do not hand this up.
This document will not be returned to the
State Examinations Commission.

Section B 180 marks

Answer **Question 1** and any other **two** questions from this section.
Question 1 is worth 80 marks. Questions 2, 3, 4 and 5 are worth 50 marks each.
Write your answers in the answerbook containing **Section A**.

Question 1
'Protein bars are a sector of the nutrition market that is rapidly expanding.' (www.tastetech.com)

The table below shows nutritional information per 100 g, for three protein bars.

	Peanut & chocolate	**Peanut & caramel**	**Crunchy peanut butter**
Energy (kcal)	492 kcal	373 kcal	518 kcal
Protein	25.6 g	36.3 g	25 g
Carbohydrates	24 g	16 g	26 g
of which sugars	15 g	3 g	16 g
Fibre	13.6 g	16.1 g	14 g
Fat	30 g	15.9 g	12 g
of which saturates	9 g	8 g	5 g
Salt	0.95 g	0.73 g	0.59 g

(a) Using the information presented in the table above, state which protein bar you would recommend for a young person who plays sport.
Give **four** reasons for your choice. (24 marks)

(b) Give an account of protein under **each** of the following headings:
- classification
- dietary sources
- functions in the body. (26 marks)

(c) Explain the importance of including water in the diet of a person who plays sport. (10 marks)

(d) Discuss **four** guidelines consumers should follow to reduce household costs when planning and purchasing food. (20 marks)

Question 2
'17% of Irish consumers are now buying better quality beef.' (*www.farmersjournal.ie*)

(a) Give an account of (i) the nutritive value and (ii) the dietetic value of meat. (20 marks)

(b) Using meat as the main ingredient, design a two-course menu suitable for the main meal of the day for a family on a low income.
Give reasons for your choice of foods. (20 marks)

(c) Describe **two** different methods of tenderising meat. (10 marks)

Question 3
Safe food preparation and storage helps to prevent food waste in Irish households.

(a) Discuss **four** kitchen hygiene practices that should be followed to ensure the safe preparation and storage of food. (16 marks)

(b) Set out the results of a study you have carried out on a refrigeration appliance.
Refer to:
- type of refrigeration appliance
- guidelines for use
- care and cleaning. (26 marks)

(c) Describe how technology has contributed to greater efficiency when planning and preparing family meals. (8 marks)

Question 4
The family home is a base that provides comfort and security for family members.

    (a) Explain how the following factors influence the family's choice when buying or renting a family home:
- family needs
- cost
- location
- trends in housing development. (20 marks)

    (b) Describe **three** advantages of having household insurance. (15 marks)

    (c) Outline **three** different ways consumers can reduce pollution to protect the environment. (15 marks)

Question 5
'Ireland has officially been recognised as one of the best places to grow old.' (*WHO*)

    (a) Discuss **four** roles and responsibilities of older people within the family. (20 marks)

    (b) **(i)** Identify **two** causes of conflict between teenagers and adults.

        (ii) Explain **two** ways of dealing with this conflict. (20 marks)

    (c) Outline **two** reasons why it is important for an older person to make a will. (10 marks)

Section C   40 or 80 marks

Answer **one** elective question **or** Question 4 (core) to include **part (a)** and either **part (b) or (c)**.
If you submitted *Textiles, Fashion and Design* coursework for examination,
you may only attempt Question 2 from this section.
Write your answer in the answerbook containing **Section A**.

Elective 1 – Home Design and Management – 80 marks

Candidates selecting this elective must answer **1(a)** and either **1(b) or 1(c)**.

1.(a) A contemporary bathroom design is shown below.

(*www.victoriaplum.com*)

- **(i)** Evaluate the suitability of the bathroom space shown above for a couple with children. (20 marks)

- **(ii)** Discuss **three** factors that should be considered when choosing a heating system for the home. (15 marks)

- **(iii)** Describe **three** guidelines to follow for the safe use of electricity in the home. (15 marks)

and

1.(b) 'A quarter of all energy used in Ireland is consumed directly in homes.' (*www.seai.ie*)

- **(i)** Describe **three** strategies that could be used to improve energy efficiency in the home. (15 marks)

- **(ii)** Name **one** renewable energy source **and** outline the advantages of the energy source named. (15 marks)

or

1.(c) (i) Describe the function of the following parts of a cold-water supply to a house:

- stop cock
- storage tank
- overflow pipe   (15 marks)

- **(ii)** Outline **three** guidelines to follow to reduce water usage in the home. (15 marks)

Elective 2 – Textiles, Fashion and Design – 40 marks

Candidates selecting this elective must answer **2(a)** and either **2(b) or 2(c)**.

2.(a) 'Music festivals bringing new trends and a boost to the fashion industry.' (*www.guardian.com*)

(*www.pinterest.com*)

    (i)   Comment on the suitability of the festival fashion shown above.
           Refer to:
- comfort
- function
- aesthetic appeal. (18 marks)

    (ii)   Describe **one** method of applying a design to a garment. (7 marks)

and

2.(b) Textiles can be treated with a variety of fabric finishes.

    (i)   Explain why fabric finishes are used on fabric. (6 marks)

    (ii)   Name **and** describe **one** fabric finish.
           Give an example of its use in clothing. (9 marks)

or

2.(c) The future of fashion is in the hands of the designers.

    (i)   Describe the contribution of Irish fashion designers to the clothing and textile industry. (9 marks)

    (ii)   Describe **two** fashion accessories currently popular with trendsetters. (6 marks)

Elective 3 – Social Studies – 80 marks

Candidates selecting this elective must answer **3(a)** and either **3(b) or 3(c)**.

3.(a) 'The unemployment rate for persons aged 15-24 is 12.4 %.' (*Oct 2022, www.cso.ie*)

    (i) Define unemployment. (6 marks)

    (ii) Discuss the effects of unemployment on:

- the individual
- the family
- society. (24 marks)

    (iii) Describe the role of education in preparing young people for the world of work. (12 marks)

    (iv) Name **and** give details of **one** statutory scheme that provides support to people who are unemployed. (8 marks)

and

3.(b) 'Primary school education supports children's learning from junior infants to sixth class.' (*NCCA*)

    (i) Describe **three** different ways primary school education contributes to the development of the individual. (15 marks)

    (ii) Discuss **three** factors that influence the educational achievement of school children. (15 marks)

or

3.(c) Ireland has undergone many social and economic changes in the past 20 years.

    (i) Discuss the impact of social and economic changes on family life.
Refer to:

- reduction in working hours
- increased participation of women in the workforce
- equal pay and employment opportunities. (15 marks)

    (ii) Outline **three** benefits of voluntary work to the community. (15 marks)

Question 4 – Core – 80 marks

Candidates selecting this question must answer **4(a)** and either **4(b)** or **4(c)**.

4.(a) 'It is estimated that up to 300,000 people in Ireland have osteoporosis.'
(*www.irishosteoporosis.ie*)

    (i)   Give an account of (i) the causes of osteoporosis **and** (ii) the effects of osteoporosis on the body.   (20 marks)

    (ii)   Evaluate **three** lifestyle and/or dietary guidelines to follow in order to prevent osteoporosis.   (15 marks)

    (iii) Discuss the role of food labelling as a source of consumer information for people following a special diet.   (15 marks)

and

4.(b) Money management is an important life skill.

    (i)   Identify **and** explain **three** factors that affect household income.   (15 marks)

    (ii)   Describe **three** benefits of setting up a family budget plan.   (15 marks)

or

4.(c) 'Family roles shape how we interact with each other in the family.' (*www.innerchange.com*)

    (i)   Discuss how the role of the adolescent has changed in the modern family.   (15 marks)

    (ii)   Explain how the family supports the physical and emotional development of children.   (15 marks)

**Do not hand this up.
This document will not be returned to the
State Examinations Commission.**

Copyright notice

This examination paper may contain text or images for which the State Examinations Commission is not the copyright owner, and which may have been adapted, for the purpose of assessment, without the authors' prior consent. This examination paper has been prepared in accordance with Section 53(5) of the *Copyright and Related Rights Act, 2000*. Any subsequent use for a purpose other than the intended purpose is not authorised. The Commission does not accept liability for any infringement of third-party rights arising from unauthorised distribution or use of this examination paper.

Leaving Certificate – Ordinary Level

Home Economics - Scientific and Social
Section B and Section C

Wednesday 7 June
Afternoon 2:00 – 4:30

Coimisiún na Scrúduithe Stáit
State Examinations Commission

Leaving Certificate Examination 2022

Home Economics – Scientific and Social

Section A and Answerbook

Ordinary Level

Wednesday 8 June Afternoon 2:00 - 4:30

200 or 240 marks

Examination Number

Day and Month of Birth

For example, 3rd February is entered as 0302

Centre Stamp

Instructions

Write your Examination Number and your Day and Month of Birth in the boxes on the front cover.

Write your answers to all parts of the examination into this answerbook. This answerbook will be scanned and your work will be presented to an examiner on screen. Anything that you write outside of the answer areas may not be seen by the examiner.

Write your answers in blue or black pen. You may use pencil for sketches, graphs and diagrams only.

There are three sections to this examination. Questions for **Sections B and C** are supplied separately but your answers must be written in this answerbook.

Section A	30 marks
	Answer **five** questions in this section.
	Each question carries 6 marks.
Section B	130 marks
	Answer **Question 1** and **one** question from questions 2, 3, 4 and 5.
	Question 1 is worth 80 marks.
	Questions 2, 3, 4 and 5 are worth 50 marks each.
Section C	40 or 80 marks
	Answer **one** elective question **or** Question 4 (core), to include **part (a)** and either **part (b)** or **part (c)**.
	If you submitted *Textiles, Fashion and Design* coursework for examination, you may only attempt Question 2 from this section.
	Electives 1 and 3 are worth 80 marks each.
	Elective 2 is worth 40 marks.
	Question 4 (core) is worth 80 marks.

Section A   **30 marks**

Answer any **five** questions from this section.
Each question carries 6 marks.
Write your answers in the spaces provided.

1. Indicate with a tick (✓) whether **each** of the following statements is true or false.

	True	False
A high salt diet can cause high blood pressure		
1 gram of fat provides 20 kilocalories of energy		
Coronary heart disease can be caused by a build-up of cholesterol on artery walls		

2. State **two** functions of lipids (fats).

(i)
(ii)

Name **one** dietary source of lipids (fats).

3. Give **one** example of **each** type of sauce listed below.

Type / Class of sauces	Example
Roux based sauce	
Egg based sauce	
Sweet sauce	

224

4. Using the words listed below, complete the following statements in relation to fruit and vegetables.

blanched   *in-season*   *vitamin C*

Citrus fruits are a rich source of _____.

Vegetables are _____ before freezing.

When vegetables are _____ they are rich in flavour.

5. Give **two** different examples of dishes cooked using the cooking methods named below.

Cooking method	Dishes	
Baking	(i)	(ii)
Grilling	(i)	(ii)

6. Outline **three** meal planning guidelines to be followed for a person recovering from illness.

(i)

(ii)

(iii)

7. Indicate with a tick (✓) whether **each** of the following statements is true or false.

	True	False
Packaging protects food from becoming damaged or contaminated		
Paper packaging is moisture proof		
All food packaging is biodegradable and recyclable		

8. Outline **three** factors that parents should consider when making food choices for preschool children.

(i)
(ii)
(iii)

9. State the guidelines that should be followed to ensure the safe preparation of food under **each** of the headings below.

Food storage
Personal hygiene
Reheating food

10. Give **one** example of **each** class of food additives.

Class of Food Additives	Example
Flavourings	
Preservatives	
Sweeteners	

11. State **two** advantages of buying goods on credit.

(i)
(ii)

Suggest **one** form of credit suitable for buying a car.

12. Indicate with a tick (✓) whether **each** of the following statements is true or false.

	True	False
Pay as you earn (PAYE) is income tax taken from a person's gross pay		
Pay Related Social Insurance (PRSI) is a compulsory deduction paid by employers and employees		
Net income is money earned before any deductions are made		

13. Outline **three** factors to be considered when choosing household textile items.

(i)
(ii)
(iii)

14. What information does **each** of the following fabric care symbols convey to the consumer?

(www.persilproclean.com)

Answerbook for Sections B and C

Instructions

Questions for **Sections B** and **C** are supplied separately.

Start each question on a new page. Write the question number in the box at the top of each page. Use the left-hand column to label each part, as shown below.

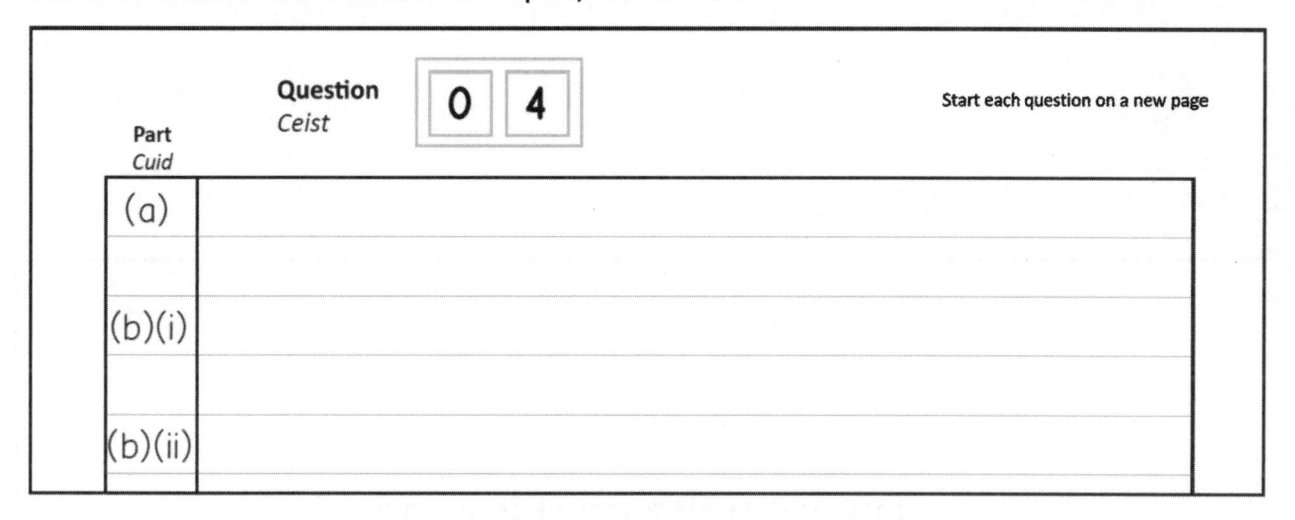

Part Cuid	Question Ceist	0	4	Start each question on a new page
(a)				
(b)(i)				
(b)(ii)				

You do not need to use all of the pages in this answerbook. If you run out of space in this answerbook, you may ask the superintendent for more paper.

Write your answers in blue or black pen. You may use pencil for sketches, graphs and diagrams only.

---

*New Format: From 2020 the returnable answerbook is provided with this section of the Exam Paper

Do not write on this page

Copyright notice
This examination paper may contain text or images for which the State Examinations Commission is not the copyright owner, and which may have been adapted, for the purpose of assessment, without the authors' prior consent. This examination paper has been prepared in accordance with *Section 53(5) of the Copyright and Related Rights Act, 2000*. Any subsequent use for a purpose other than the intended purpose is not authorised. The Commission does not accept liability for any infringement of third-party rights arising from unauthorised distribution or use of this examination paper.

Leaving Certificate – Ordinary Level

Home Economics – Scientific and Social
Section A and Answerbook

Wednesday 8 June
Afternoon 2:00 - 4:30

2022. M47

2022L098G2EL

Coimisiún na Scrúduithe Stáit
State Examinations Commission

LEAVING CERTIFICATE EXAMINATION 2022

Home Economics – Scientific and Social

ORDINARY LEVEL

Section B and Section C

WEDNESDAY 8 JUNE   AFTERNOON 2:00 – 4:30

Section B 130 marks
Answer **Question 1** and **one** question from questions 2, 3, 4 and 5.
Question 1 is worth 80 marks.
Questions 2, 3, 4 and 5 are worth 50 marks each.

Section C 40 or 80 marks
Answer **one** elective question **or** Question 4 (core), to include **part (a)** and either **part (b) or part (c)**.

If you submitted *Textiles, Fashion and Design* coursework for examination, you may only attempt Question 2 from this section.

Electives 1 and 3 are worth 80 marks each.
Elective 2 is worth 40 marks.
Question 4 (core) is worth 80 marks.

Do not hand this up.
This document will not be returned to the
State Examinations Commission.

Section B — 130 marks

Answer **Question 1** and **one** question from questions 2, 3, 4 and 5.
Question 1 is worth 80 marks. Questions 2, 3, 4 and 5 are worth 50 marks each.
Write your answers in the answerbook containing **Section A**.

Question 1
'Milk is a staple food in the diets of Irish children.' (*www.nationaldairycouncil.ie*)

The table below shows the nutritional content of whole milk and super milk fat-free per 100 ml.

Type of Milk	Energy (kcal)	Protein	Carbohydrates	Fat	Calcium	Vitamin B12
Whole Milk	64 kcal	3.4 g	4.7 g	3.5 g	119 mg	0.4 µg
Super Milk Fat-free	35 kcal	3.3 g	5.0 g	0.2 g	160 mg	0.4 µg

(*www.avonmore.ie*)

(a) Using the information presented in the table above, state which milk you would recommend for a teenager.
Give **four** reasons for your choice. (20 marks)

(b) Outline **three** interesting ways of including dairy products in a teenager's diet. (12 marks)

(c) Give an account of calcium under **each** of the following headings:
- functions in the body
- dietary sources
- effect of deficiency. (28 marks)

(d) Discuss **four** factors to be considered when buying **and** storing dairy products in order to reduce food waste. (20 marks)

Question 2

'Six in ten primary school children are not eating enough fibre.' (www.bordbia.ie)

(a) Give an account of **(i)** the nutritive value **and (ii)** the dietetic value of cereals. (20 marks)

(b) Plan a high fibre menu (3 meals, to include a packed lunch) for one day for a school-going child. (18 marks)

(c) Outline the effects of heat on cereals. (12 marks)

Question 3

Home food preservation helps to reduce food waste.

(a) Give an account of **one** method of home food preservation.
Refer to:
- name of preservation method
- suitable foods
- steps to carry out the method of preservation. (24 marks)

(b) Describe **four** safety guidelines to follow when preserving food in the home. (16 marks)

(c) State **two** ways food labelling benefits the consumer when purchasing processed foods. (10 marks)

Question 4
'When you buy a product or a service you have a number of rights under Irish legislation.'
(*www.citizensinformation.ie*)

    (a)   Name **and** explain **four** consumer rights when buying household appliances. (16 marks)

    (b)   Set out the results of a study you have carried out on a small electrical kitchen appliance. Refer to:
- type of appliance
- guidelines for use
- guidelines for care and cleaning. (24 marks)

    (c)   Explain **two** benefits to the consumer of the EU energy label on electrical appliances. (10 marks)

Question 5
Marriage is a popular lifestyle choice for couples in Irish society.

    (a)   Discuss the rights **and** responsibilities of a couple within a marriage relationship. (20 marks)

    (b)   Give an account of the following options available to married couples who are separating:
- legal separation
- divorce. (20 marks)

    (c)   Describe **two** different cultural variations in marital arrangements. (10 marks)

Section C   40 or 80 marks

Answer **one** elective question **or** Question 4 (core) to include **part (a)** and either **part (b) or (c)**.
If you submitted *Textiles, Fashion and Design* coursework for examination,
you may only attempt Question 2 from this section.
Write your answer in the answerbook containing **Section A**.

Elective 1 – Home Design and Management – 80 marks
Candidates selecting this elective must answer **1(a)** and either **1(b) or 1(c)**.

1.(a) A popular open plan kitchen/living space is shown below.

(*www.roomsketcher.com*)

(i) Evaluate the suitability of this kitchen/living space for a family with children. (20 marks)

(ii) Discuss **three** factors that should be considered when planning a lighting system for an open plan kitchen/living room. (15 marks)

(iii) Give details of **three** types of contemporary lighting in the home. (15 marks)

and

1.(b) 'As people get older, they often spend more time in their homes.' (*Age Friendly Ireland*)

(i) Discuss **three** factors that influence the choice of housing for an older person.
(15 marks)

(ii) Outline **three** ways an older person can reduce their home energy bills.
(15 marks)

or

1.(c) 'Electricity can be dangerous if not used properly.' (*www.safeelectric.ie*)

(i) Describe how the following electrical safety devices provide protection when using electricity in the home.

(a) miniature circuit breakers   (b) earth wire.   (10 marks)

(ii) Outline **four** guidelines to follow for the safe use of electricity in the home. (20 marks)

Elective 2 – Textiles, Fashion and Design – 40 marks

Candidates selecting this elective must answer **2(a)** and either **2(b)** or **2(c)**.

2.(a) 'Athleisure wear is the fashion trend that can be worn anywhere anytime.' (*www.squatwolf.com*)

(*www.pinterest.com*)

- (i) Comment on the suitability of the athleisure wear outfits shown above. Refer to:
    - comfort
    - function
    - design features. (18 marks)

- (ii) Suggest **one** accessory that could enhance the appeal of the athleisurewear outfits **and** give a reason for your choice. (7 marks)

and

2.(b) Man-made fabrics have many uses including clothing, household items and industrial products.

- (i) Write a profile of **one** man-made fabric under **each** of the following headings:
    - how the fabric is constructed
    - properties. (9 marks)

- (ii) Give **two** advantages of using man-made fibres/fabric in everyday wear. (6 marks)

or

2.(c) Wardrobes are bulging, yet we continue to buy more clothes.

- (i) Discuss **three** factors that influence teenagers' clothing choices. (9 marks)

- (ii) Evaluate how social media contributes to current fashion trends. (6 marks)

Elective 3 – Social Studies – 80 marks

Candidates selecting this elective must answer **3(a)** and either **3(b) or 3(c)**.

3.(a) 'A quarter of those in poverty are children.' (*Social Justice Ireland, 2021*)

    (i) Define 'poverty'.

    Explain **each** of the following:
- relative poverty
- absolute poverty. (16 marks)

    (ii) Describe **four** reasons why poverty continues to be a feature in modern Irish society. (20 marks)

    (iii) Name **and** give details of **one** voluntary organisation that provides support to families at risk of poverty. (14 marks)

and

3.(b) 'Communities are the life blood of rural Ireland.' (*www.gov.ie*)

    (i) Discuss **three** reasons why people are moving from rural areas to urban areas. (15 marks)

    (ii) Explain how the movement of people from rural areas to urban areas has impacted family life. (15 marks)

or

3.(c) 'Deciding on childcare is a big decision for any parent.' (*www.citizensinformation.ie*)

    (i) Give an account of **three** factors parents should consider when choosing a childcare facility for their child. (15 marks)

    (ii) Describe how attending pre-school can promote a child's development. (15 marks)

Question 4 – Core – 80 marks

Candidates selecting this question must answer **4(a)** and either **4(b) or 4(c)**.

4.(a) 'Fish has a reputation for being one of the healthiest foods we can eat.' (*www.bbc.com*)

   (i) Give an account of (i) the nutritive value **and** (ii) the dietetic value of fish. (20 marks)

   (ii) Outline:
   - the guidelines to follow when buying fresh fish
   - the effects of cooking on fish. (18 marks)

   (iii) Name **one** method of processing fish to extend its shelf life and give **one** advantage and **one** disadvantage of the method named. (12 marks)

and

4.(b) Retailers use a variety of techniques to increase consumer spending.

   (i) Give details of **three** ways retailers can encourage consumers to purchase goods. (15 marks)

   (ii) Outline the procedure a consumer should follow when making a complaint about a faulty product. (15 marks)

or

4.(c) The successful organisation of the family unit depends on good management skills.

   (i) Discuss how the following factors may affect the management of the home:
   - dual roles
   - stages in life cycle
   - employment patterns. (15 marks)

   (ii) Describe **three** ways in which technology has contributed to the efficient management of the home. (15 marks)

Do not hand this up.
This document will not be returned to the State Examinations Commission.

Copyright notice
This examination paper may contain text or images for which the State Examinations Commission is not the copyright owner, and which may have been adapted, for the purpose of assessment, without the authors' prior consent. This examination paper has been prepared in accordance with Section 53(5) of the Copyright and Related Rights Act, (2000). Any subsequent use for a purpose other than the intended purpose is not authorised. The Commission does not accept liability for any infringement of third-party rights arising from unauthorised distribution or use of this examination paper.

Leaving Certificate – Ordinary Level

Home Economics - Scientific and Social
Section B and Section C

Wednesday 8 June
Afternoon 2:00 – 4:30

2021. M47

2021L098G1EL

Comisiún na Scrúduithe Stáit
State Examinations Commission

Leaving Certificate Examination 2021

Home Economics – Scientific and Social

Section A and Answerbook

Ordinary Level

Wednesday 9 June - Afternoon 2:00 – 4:30

200 or 240 marks

Examination Number

Day and Month of Birth

For example, 3rd February is entered as 0302

Centre Stamp

Instructions

Write your Examination Number and your Day and Month of Birth in the boxes on the front cover.

Write your answers to all parts of the examination into this answerbook.

Write your answers in blue or black pen. You may use pencil for sketches, graphs and diagrams only.

There are three sections to this examination. Questions for **Sections B and C** are supplied separately but your answers must be written in this answerbook.

Section A   30 marks
Answer any **five** questions in this section.
Each question carries 6 marks.

Section B   130 marks
Answer **Question 1** and **one** question from questions 2, 3, 4 and 5.
Question 1 is worth 80 marks.
Questions 2, 3, 4 and 5 are worth 50 marks each.

Section C   40 or 80 marks
Answer **one** elective question **or** question 4 (core) to include **part (a)** and either **part (b) or (c)**.

If you submitted *Textiles, Fashion and Design* coursework for examination, you may only attempt Question 2 from this section.

Electives 1 and 3 are worth 80 marks each.
Elective 2 is worth 40 marks.
Question 4 (core) is worth 80 marks.

Section A   30 marks

Answer any **five** questions from this section.
Each question carries 6 marks.
Write your answers in the spaces provided.

1. Indicate with a tick (✓) whether **each** of the following statements is true or false.

	True	False
Meat contains high biological value protein		
Proteins are large molecules made up of smaller units called amino acids		
Sugar is a source of protein		

2. Using the words listed below, complete the following statements in relation to minerals.

   calcium   *osteoporosis*   *iron*

   A deficiency of calcium in the diet can cause _____.

   Vitamin C assists in _____ absorption.

   Cheese is a good dietary source of _____.

3. Outline **one** cause of toughness in meat.

   Name **two** methods of tenderising meat.

(i)
(ii)

4. Indicate with a tick (✓) whether **each** of the following statements is true or false.

	True	False
Peas, beans and lentils are pulse vegetables		
Fruit and vegetables do not contain fibre		
Vegetables have a high water content		

5. Outline **three** healthy eating guidelines for children.

(i)
(ii)
(iii)

6. Indicate with a tick (✓) whether **each** of the following statements is true or false.

	True	False
Food is processed to extend its shelf life		
An example of cross contamination is the transfer of bacteria from raw to cooked food		
Cooking food at 50°C kills all bacteria		

7. Listed below are **three** types of flour. Give **one** different culinary use of each.

Type of flour	Culinary use
Self-raising flour	
Wholemeal flour	
Plain white flour (cream)	

243

8. Indicate with a tick (✓) whether **each** of the following statements is true or false.

	True	False
Periodontal/gum disease affects the tissues surrounding the teeth		
A lacto-vegetarian does not eat dairy produce		
A high fibre diet reduces the risk of bowel disease		

9. Match the method of food preservation with the correct definition.

Heat treatment   Dehydration   Freezing

Definition	Method of food preservation
Boiling fruit, vegetables or a mixture of both with sugar, vinegar and spices	
Using very low temperatures which are unsuitable for enzyme activity and microbial growth	
Preserves food by removing moisture	

10. Give **two** advantages of private health insurance.

(i)
(ii)

Suggest **one** method of payment that could be used to purchase private health insurance.

11. Outline **two** factors that should be considered when choosing electrical appliances.

(i)
(ii)

How can electrical appliances be disposed of to avoid damage to the environment?

12. Outline **three** different uses of textiles in the home.

(i)
(ii)
(iii)

13. In relation to household expenditure, explain **each** of the following:

Essential expenditure
Discretionary expenditure

14. What information does **each** of the following fabric care symbols convey to the consumer?

www.woolmark.com

www.omo.com

Answerbook for Sections B and C

Instructions

Questions for **Sections B** and **C** are supplied separately.

Start each question on a new page. Write the question number in the box at the top of each page. Use the left-hand column to label each part, as shown below.

Part *Cuid*	**Question** **0 4** *Ceist*	**Start each question on a new page** *Cuir tús le gach ceist ar leathanach nua*
(a)		
(b)(i)		
(b)(ii)		

You do not need to use all of the pages in this answerbook. If you run out of space in this answerbook, you may ask the superintendent for more paper.

Write your answers in blue or black pen. You may use pencil for sketches, graphs and diagrams only.

*New Format: From 2020 the returnable answerbook is provided with this section of the Exam Paper

For examiner use only	
1. Total of end of page totals	
2. Aggregate total of all disallowed questions(s)	
3. Total mark awarded (1 minus 2)	

Question	Marks Examiner	Adv Examiner
Total		
Grand Total		

Copyright notice

This examination paper may contain text or images for which the State Examinations Commission is not the copyright owner, and which may have been adapted, for the purpose of assessment, without the authors' prior consent. This examination paper has been prepared in accordance with Section 53(5) of the *Copyright and Related Rights Act, 2000*. Any subsequent use for a purpose other than the intended purpose is not authorised. The Commission does not accept liability for any infringement of third-party rights arising from unauthorised distribution or use of this examination paper.

Leaving Certificate – Ordinary Level

Home Economics – Scientific and Social
Section A and Answer book

Wednesday 9 June
Afternoon 2:00 – 4:30

2021. M47

2021L098G2EL

Coimisiún na Scrúduithe Stáit
State Examinations Commission

LEAVING CERTIFICATE EXAMINATION 2021

Home Economics – Scientific and Social

ORDINARY LEVEL

Section B and Section C

WEDNESDAY 9 JUNE   **AFTERNOON 2:00 – 4:30**

Section B   130 marks
Answer **Question 1** and **one** question from questions 2, 3, 4 and 5.
Question 1 is worth 80 marks.
Questions 2, 3, 4 and 5 are worth 50 marks each.

Section C   40 or 80 marks
Answer **one** elective question **or** question 4 (core) to include **part (a)** and either **part (b) or (c)**.

If you submitted *Textiles, Fashion and Design* coursework for examination, you may only attempt Question 2 from this section.

Electives 1 and 3 are worth 80 marks each.
Elective 2 is worth 40 marks.
Question 4 (core) is worth 80 marks.

Do not hand this up

# Section B	130 marks

Answer **Question 1** and **one** question from questions 2, 3, 4 and 5.
Question 1 is worth 80 marks. Questions 2, 3, 4 and 5 are worth 50 marks each.
Write your answers in the answerbook containing **Section A**.

Question 1
'More than a quarter of young people growing up in Ireland are obese or overweight according to the latest *Growing Up in Ireland* survey.' (www.irish examiner.com)

The table below shows nutritional information per 100 g, for full fat, low fat and fat free natural yoghurt.

	Full fat natural yoghurt	Low fat natural yoghurt	Fat free natural yoghurt
Energy (kcal)	133 kcal	65 kcal	54 kcal
Fat
of which saturates	9.4 g
5.5 g	1.8 g
1.1 g	0.4 g
0.2 g
Carbohydrates
of which sugars	5.9 g
3.2 g	6.9 g
6.8 g	7.6 g
7.3 g
Fibre	0.3 g	0.5 g	0.5 g
Protein	6.0 g	4.8 g	4.8 g
Salt	0.20 g	0.20 g	0.19 g

(a) Using the information presented in the table, state which of the yoghurts you would recommend for an obese person.
Give **four** reasons for your choice.   (20 marks)

(b) State **three** causes of obesity.   (12 marks)

(c) Give an account of lipids (fats) under **each** of the following headings:
   - classification
   - functions in the body
   - dietary sources.   (28 marks)

(d) Discuss **four** factors to be considered when selecting **and** buying foods to reduce fat intake in the diet.   (20 marks)

Question 2
Healthy eating during pregnancy is critical to the baby's growth and development.

    (a) Discuss **four** dietary requirements of pregnant women. (20 marks)

    (b) Having regard to current healthy eating guidelines, set out a menu (3 meals) for one day for a pregnant woman. (18 marks)

    (c) Explain how food labelling assist consumers when buying food. (12 marks)

Question 3
Irish grown vegetables get to our shelves quickly, and so are more nutritious.

    (a) Give an account of **(i)** the nutritive value **and (ii)** the dietetic value of vegetables. (20 marks)

    (b) Outline:
        (i) the effects of cooking on vegetables
        (ii) the guidelines for storing vegetables. (18 marks)

    (c) Suggest **two** interesting ways of including vegetables in the diet of children. (12 marks)

Question 4
Good money management is an important life skill.

    (a)   Discuss **four** advantages of planning a household budget for a family.   (20 marks)

    (b)   Set out a weekly budget plan for a family (two adults and two children) with a net income of €800 a week.   (20 marks)

    (c)   State **one** advantage and **one** disadvantage of buying goods on credit.   (10 marks)

Question 5
We live in an increasingly diverse world, even within our own family structures.

    (a)   Describe **each** of the following family structures:
- one parent family
- nuclear family
- blended family.   (18 marks)

    (b)   Discuss the roles **and** responsibilities of adolescents/teenagers within a family.   (20 marks)

    (c)   Outline why good communication is important between family members.   (12 marks)

Section C   **40 or 80 marks**

Answer **one** elective question **or** question 4 (core) to include **part (a)** and either **part (b)** or **(c)**.
If you submitted *Textiles, Fashion and Design* coursework for examination,
you may only attempt Question 2 from this section.
Write your answer in the answerbook containing **Section A**.

Elective 1 – Home Design and Management – 80 marks

Candidates selecting this elective must answer **1(a)** and either **1(b)** or **1(c)**.

1.(a) The diagram below shows the average heat loss for a family home.

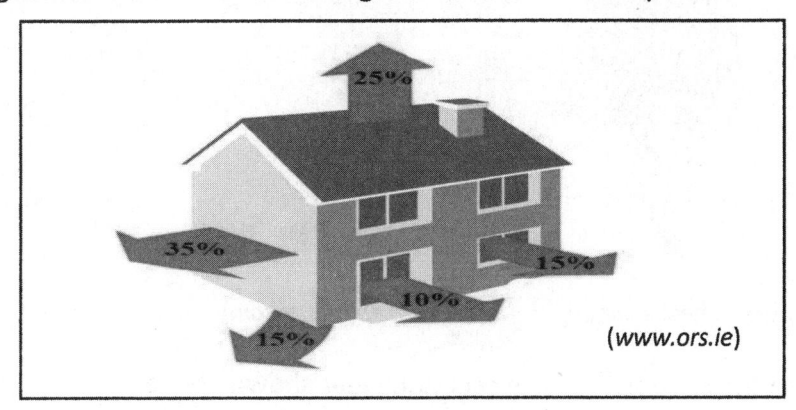

(www.ors.ie)

- **(i)** State **four** advantages of having a house well insulated. (20 marks)

- **(ii)** Name **and** describe the method of insulation you would recommend for **each** of the following:

  (a) attic   **(b)** walls   **(c)** windows. (15 marks)

- **(iii)** State the advantages **and/or** the disadvantages of solar energy. (15 marks)

and

1.(b) Buying a first home is an exciting adventure.

- **(i)** State the advantages **and** the disadvantages of buying a home of your own. (12 marks)

- **(ii)** Discuss how the housing requirements of a family with children may differ from that of a person living on their own. (18 marks)

or

1.(c) Interior designers help people create their dream home.

- **(i)** Discuss **three** factors to be considered when planning the interior design of a house. (15 marks)

- **(ii)** Explain how soft furnishings can enhance the overall appearance of a room. (15 marks)

Elective 2 – Textiles, Fashion and Design – 40 marks

Candidates selecting this elective must answer **2(a)** and either **2(b) or 2(c)**.

2.(a) 'Fashions fade, style is eternal.' (*Yves Saint Laurent*)

(*www.pinterest.com*)   (*www.theblacktux.com*)

(i) Comment on the suitability of the occasion wear shown above.

Refer to:

(a) shape (b) comfort (c) design features. (18 marks)

(ii) Suggest **one** accessory you could add to enhance either of the above outfits. Give **one** reason for your choice. (7 marks)

and

2.(b) Today's consumers are willing to pay more for clothing produced with natural fabrics.

(i) Write a profile of a natural fabric under **each** of the following headings:
- how the fabric is constructed
- properties. (9 marks)

(ii) Give **two** advantages of using natural fibres/fabric in everyday wear. (6 marks)

or

2.(c) Irish fashion is thriving on the international stage.

(i) Explain how **each** of the following factors may influence a person's choice of clothing.

(a) function (b) money available (c) cultural influences. (9 marks)

(ii) Discuss the contribution of trendsetters/bloggers to current fashion trends. (6 marks)

Elective 3 – Social Studies – 80 marks

Candidates selecting this elective must answer **3(a)** and either **3(b) or 3(c)**.

3.(a) Education for a child begins at home and is a lifelong process.

- (i) Outline how education contributes to the development of the individual.
  Refer to **each** of the following:
  - physical development
  - emotional development
  - intellectual development. (18 marks)

- (ii) Give an account of **four** factors that influence the educational achievement of school children. (20 marks)

- (iii) Explain **three** benefits to students of participating in work experience while in second level school. (12 marks)

and

3.(b) 'Physical activity plays an important role in the lives of children and young people.'
(www.education.ie)

- (i) Discuss **three** reasons why leisure is important in today's society. (15 marks)

- (ii) Describe how a person's choice of leisure activities are influenced by **each** of the following:
  - cost
  - occupation
  - age. (15 marks)

or

3.(c) The impact of unemployment can be long lasting.

- (i) Discuss the effects of unemployment on:
  - young individuals
  - the family
  - society. (18 marks)

- (ii) Name **and** give details of **one** voluntary organisation that provides support to the unemployed. (12 marks)

Question 4 – Core – 80 marks

Candidates selecting this question must answer **4(a)** and either **4(b) or 4(c)**.

4.(a) The ultimate convenience food, eggs are powerhouses of nutrition.
(*www.bbcgoodfood.com*)

  (i) Give an account of (i) the nutritive value **and** (ii) the dietetic value of eggs. (20 marks)

  (ii) Outline:
  - different ways of including eggs in the diet
  - the effects of heat on eggs. (18 marks)

  (iii) Give **three** reasons for the growing popularity of goods supplied by small Irish food producers. (12 marks)

and

4.(b) 'Consumers want to hear about discounts and sales, not just products.'
(*www.retail-week.com*)

  (i) Discuss how the following might affect consumers' decision making when shopping:
  - household income
  - discount offers
  - shopper loyalty schemes. (15 marks)

  (ii) State the advantages **and** the disadvantages of online shopping. (15 marks)

or

4.(c) The goal of conflict resolution is not to decide who is right or wrong.

  (i) Identify **three** factors which may influence an adolescent's/teenager's behaviour. (15 marks)

  (ii) Discuss **three** aspects of adolescent/teenager's behaviour that may lead to conflict in the home. (15 marks)

Do not hand this up

Copyright notice
This examination paper may contain text or images for which the State Examinations Commission is not the copyright owner, and which may have been adapted, for the purpose of assessment, without the authors' prior consent. This examination paper has been prepared in accordance with Section 53(5) of the Copyright and Related Rights Act, 2000. Any subsequent use for a purpose other than the intended purpose is not authorised. The Commission does not accept liability for any infringement of third-party rights arising from unauthorised distribution or use of this examination paper.

2021 OL

Leaving Certificate – Ordinary Level

Home Economics - Scientific and Social
Section B and Section C

Wednesday 9 June
Afternoon 2:00 – 4:30

2020.M47

2020L098G1EL

Coimisiún na Scrúduithe Stáit
State Examinations Commission

Leaving Certificate Examination 2020
Home Economics – Scientific and Social

Section A and Answerbook

Ordinary Level

2 hours 30 minutes

280 or 320 marks

Examination Number

Day and Month of Birth

For example, 3rd February is entered as 0302

Centre Stamp

Instructions

Write your Examination Number and your Day and Month of Birth in the boxes on the front cover.

Write your answers to all parts of the examination into this answerbook. This answerbook will be scanned and your work will be presented to an examiner on screen. Anything that you write outside of the answer areas may not be seen by the examiner.

Write your answers in blue or black pen. You may use pencil for sketches, graphs and diagrams only.

There are three sections to this examination. Questions for **Sections B and C** are supplied separately but your answers must be written in this answerbook.

Section A 60 marks
Answer **ten** questions in this section.
Each question carries 6 marks.

Section B 180 marks
Answer **Question 1** and any other **two** questions.
Question 1 is worth 80 marks.
Questions 2, 3, 4, and 5 are worth 50 marks each.

Section C 40 or 80 marks
Answer **one** elective question, to include **part (a)** and either **part (b) or (c)**.

If you submitted *Textiles, Fashion and Design* coursework for examination, you may only attempt Question 2 from this section.

Electives 1 and 3 are worth 80 marks each.
Elective 2 is worth 40 marks.

Section A   **60 marks**

Answer any **ten** questions from this section.
Each question carries 6 marks.
Write your answers in the spaces provided.

1. Indicate with a tick (✓) whether **each** of the following statements is true or false.

	True	False
Carbohydrates are a source of heat and energy		
Carbohydrates contain the element nitrogen		
Excess carbohydrates are converted to fat in the body		

2. Explain the following properties of lipids (fats):

(i) Smoke point
(ii) Flash point

3. Using the words listed below, complete the following statements in relation to milk processing.

spray drying   pasteurised   homogenisation

Milk is _____ to make it safe for human consumption.

The process that breaks down fat globules in milk is called _____.

_____ is used to change liquid milk into milk powder.

4. Name **two** culinary uses of eggs and suggest a food/dish that demonstrates **each** culinary use.

Culinary use of eggs	Food/dish

5. Indicate with a tick (✓) whether **each** of the following statements is true or false.

	True	False
A *roux* based sauce is made of equal quantities of fat and flour		
Sauces improve the nutritive value of a dish		
Sauces should only be served hot		

6. Explain the term *'food additive'*.

Name **two** food additives used in processed foods.

(i)
(ii)

7. State the effect on the body of **each** of the following:

	Effect on the body
High saturated fat diet	
Low dietary fibre diet	
Low calcium intake	

8. Name **two** foods exported from Ireland.

(i)
(ii)

List **two** career opportunities in the food industry.

(i)
(ii)

9. Indicate with a (✓) whether **each** of the following statements is true or false.

	True	False
Universal Social Charge (USC) is a voluntary deduction from wages or salaries		
Utility bills are an example of essential expenditure		
Child benefit is a universal social welfare payment		

10. State **two** advantages of online shopping.

(i)
(ii)

Name **one** method of paying for goods online.

11. Outline **three** factors that influence a family's choice of housing.

(i)
(ii)
(iii)

12. Explain **each** of the textile care symbols below.

(www.goodhousekeeping.com)

Answerbook for Sections B and C

Instructions

Questions for **Sections B** and **C** are supplied separately.

Start each question on a new page. Write the question number in the box at the top of each page. Use the left-hand column to label each part, as shown below.

Part Cuid	Question Ceist 0 4	Start each question on a new page *Cuir tús le gach ceist ar leathanach nua*
(a)		
(b)(i)		
(b)(ii)		

You do not need to use all of the pages in this answerbook. If you run out of space in this answerbook, you may ask the superintendent for more paper.

Write your answers in blue or black pen. You may use pencil for sketches, graphs and diagrams only.

*New Format: From 2020 the returnable answerbook is provided with this section of the Exam Paper

Do not write on this page

Copyright notice
This examination paper may contain text or images for which the State Examinations Commission is not the copyright owner, and which may have been adapted, for the purpose of assessment, without the authors' prior consent. This examination paper has been prepared in accordance with Section 53(5) of the Copyright and Related Rights Act, 2000. Any subsequent use for a purpose other than the intended purpose is not authorised. The Commission does not accept liability for any infringement of third-party rights arising from unauthorised distribution or use of this examination paper.

Leaving Certificate – Ordinary Level

Home Economics – Scientific and Social
Section A and Answerbook

2 hours 30 minutes

2020. M47

2020L098G2EL

Coimisiún na Scrúduithe Stáit
State Examinations Commission

LEAVING CERTIFICATE EXAMINATION 2020

Home Economics – Scientific and Social

ORDINARY LEVEL

Section B and Section C

2 hours 30 minutes

Section B	180 marks Answer **Question 1** and any other **two** questions. Question 1 is worth 80 marks. Questions 2, 3, 4, and 5 are worth 50 marks each.
Section C	40 or 80 marks Answer **one** elective question, to include **part (a)** and either **part (b) or (c)**. If you submitted *Textiles, Fashion and Design* coursework for examination, you may only attempt Question 2 from this section. Electives 1 and 3 are worth 80 marks each. Elective 2 is worth 40 marks.

Do not hand this up

Section B   180 marks

Answer **Question 1** and any other **two questions** from this section.
Question 1 is worth 80 marks. Questions 2, 3, 4, and 5 are worth 50 marks each.
Write your answer in the answerbook containing **Section A**.

Question 1

'1 in 3 people claim to have reduced the intake of red meat in their diet.'

(Dietary Lifestyles Report | Thinking House, Bord Bia)

The table below shows the reasons why people are reducing their intake of red meat.

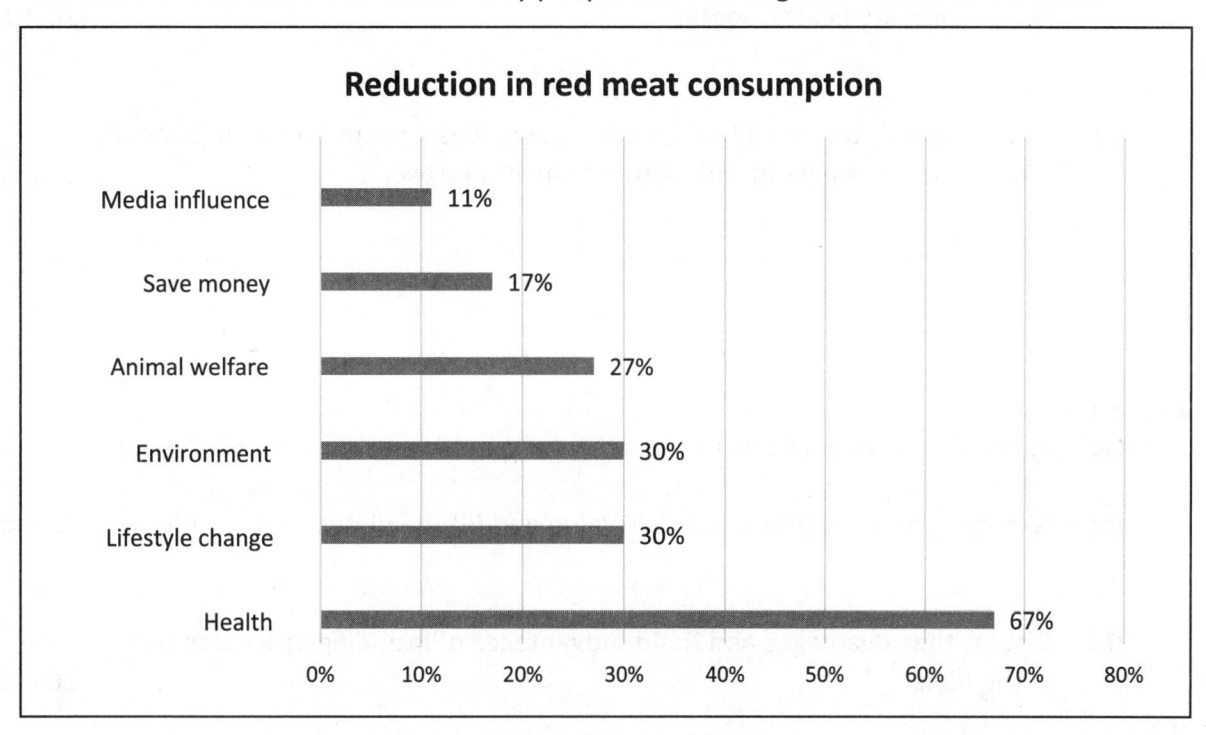

Reduction in red meat consumption

Reason	%
Media influence	11%
Save money	17%
Animal welfare	27%
Environment	30%
Lifestyle change	30%
Health	67%

(a) (i) Using the information provided in the table, comment on **four** of the reasons why people are choosing to reduce their intake of red meat. (24 marks)

(ii) Name a protein food that could be used instead of red meat. (6 marks)

(b) Give an account of iron under **each** of the following headings:
- functions in the body
- dietary sources
- effect of deficiency. (24 marks)

(c) State **two** ways of increasing iron in the diet. (6 marks)

(d) Discuss **four** factors consumers should consider when selecting **and** buying meat and meat products. (20 marks)

Question 2
'Cardiovascular disease including coronary heart disease is the most common cause of death in Ireland, accounting for 36% of all deaths.' (*www.hse.ie*)

    (a)   **(i)**   Explain *coronary heart disease* (CHD).

          (ii)   Outline **three** factors that increase a person's risk of developing coronary heart disease.   (16 marks)

    (b)   State **four** healthy eating guidelines that should be followed to reduce the risk of coronary heart disease.   (16 marks)

    (c)   Having regard to current healthy eating guidelines, set out a menu (3 meals) for one day for a person with coronary heart disease.   (18 marks)

Question 3
'Fish has long been recognised as one of nature's healthiest foods.'   (*www.bordbia.ie*)

    (a)   Give an account of **(i)** the nutritive value **and (ii)** the dietetic value of fish.   (20 marks)

    (b)   Discuss the advantages **and** the disadvantages of including processed fish in the diet.   (16 marks)

    (c)   Name **two** food packaging materials.
          Outline the impact of **each** packaging material on the environment.   (14 marks)

Question 4

Microwave ovens are popular kitchen appliances.

(a) Discuss **four** factors that should be considered when selecting kitchen appliances.

(16 marks)

(b) Outline **three** consumer responsibilities. (12 marks)

(c) Set out the results of a study you have carried out on a microwave oven.

Refer to:
- guidelines for use
- modern features
- care and cleaning. (22 marks)

Question 5

'In Ireland there were 21,053 marriages in 2018 including 664 same-sex marriages.' (*www.cso.ie*)

(a) (i) Define '*marriage*'.

(ii) Outline **four** conditions necessary for a marriage to be legally valid in Ireland.

(25 marks)

(b) Discuss **three** benefits to a couple of attending a pre-marriage course. (15 marks)

(c) Explain **each** of the following options available to couples who are experiencing difficulties in their marriage:
- marriage counselling
- legal separation. (10 marks)

Section C — 40 or 80 marks

Answer **one elective question** from this section.
If you submitted *Textiles, Fashion and Design* coursework for examination,
you may only attempt Question 2 from this section.
Write your answer in the answerbook containing **Section A**.

Elective 1 – Home Design and Management – 80 marks

Candidates selecting this elective must answer **1(a)** and either **1(b)** or **1(c)**.

1.(a) Shown below is the ground floor plan of a house.

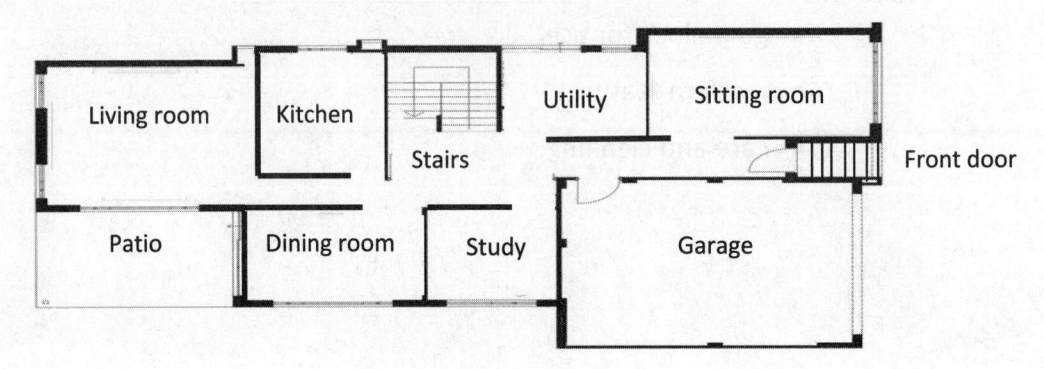

[Floor plan showing: Living room, Kitchen, Stairs, Utility, Sitting room, Front door, Patio, Dining room, Study, Garage]

- **(i)** Evaluate the suitability of the floor plan layout for the daily living requirements of a family. *(20 marks)*

- **(ii)** Give details of **two** modifications that could be made to the floor plan layout to suit the requirements of people with disabilities. *(10 marks)*

- **(iii)** Name **and** describe **two** professional services available to people when designing and building a home. *(10 marks)*

- **(iv)** Identify **and** comment on **two** trends currently popular in interior design. *(10 marks)*

and

1.(b) Good ventilation is very important to home comfort.

- **(i)** Outline the importance of good ventilation in the home. *(12 marks)*

- **(ii)** Name **two** methods of ventilation suitable for a bathroom. Explain the underlying principle of **each** method of ventilation named. *(18 marks)*

or

1.(c) There is a whole world of wall finishes to explore.

- **(i)** Discuss **four** factors to consider when selecting wall finishes for a home. *(16 marks)*

- **(ii)** Name **one** wall finish suitable for a kitchen. State **one** advantage **and one** disadvantage of the wall finish named. *(14 marks)*

Elective 2 – Textiles, Fashion and Design – 40 marks

Candidates selecting this elective must answer **2(a) and either 2(b) or 2(c)**.

2.(a) Children's clothing has become as fashionable as adult clothing in recent years.

(*www.dunnesstores.com*)

- **(i)** Comment on the suitability of the children's clothing shown above.

    Refer to:
    - function
    - comfort
    - aesthetic appeal. (18 marks)

- **(ii)** Name **one** fabric suitable for a child's trousers/pants **and** give a reason for your choice. (7 marks)

and

2.(b) Bloggers, influencers and *YouTube* sensations are some of the modern world's trendsetters.

- **(i)** Explain how trendsetters influence the choice of clothing worn by young adults. (9 marks)

- **(ii)** Name **and** describe **one** method of colour application suitable for natural fabrics. (6 marks)

or

2.(c) The Irish fashion industry is hugely exciting with lots of emerging talent.

- **(i)** Discuss the role of small businesses in the clothing and textile industry in Ireland. (9 marks)

- **(ii)** Give details of **one** career opportunity in the fashion industry. (6 marks)

Elective 3 – Social Studies – 80 marks

Candidates selecting this elective must answer **3(a)** and either **3(b)** or **3(c)**.

3.(a) A strong work ethic is an important part of being successful in a person's career.

  (i) Define *work* and *work ethic*. (6 marks)

  (ii) Discuss **four** factors that influence a person's attitude to work. (20 marks)

  (iii) Outline the benefits of voluntary work to the volunteer **and** to the community. (16 marks)

  (iv) Name **and** give details of **one** support provided by voluntary organisations to individuals and families in need. (8 marks)

and

3.(b) 'Childminding is of huge importance to children, to parents, to our economy and to our society.'

  (i) Discuss **four** factors parents should consider when choosing suitable childcare for their children. (16 marks)

  (ii) Identify **and** describe **two** childcare options available to a family with young children. (14 marks)

or

3.(c) Irish society is changing rapidly and these changes are having a significant impact on the family.

  (i) Outline the impact (effect) of **each** of the following on family life:
  - reduction in working hours
  - improved conditions of work
  - improvements in the provision of education. (18 marks)

  (ii) Explain how the Working Family Payment (*Family Income Supplement*) provides support to families. (12 marks)

Do not hand this up

Copyright notice
This examination paper may contain text or images for which the State Examinations Commission is not the copyright owner, and which may have been adapted, for the purpose of assessment, without the authors' prior consent. This examination paper has been prepared in accordance with Section 53(5) of the Copyright and Related Rights Act, 2000. Any subsequent use for a purpose other than the intended purpose is not authorised. The Commission does not accept liability for any infringement of third-party rights arising from unauthorised distribution or use of this examination paper.

2020 OL

Leaving Certificate – Ordinary Level

Home Economics - Scientific and Social
Section B and Section C

2 hours 30 minutes

2019. M47

Write your Examination Number here

2019L098G1EL

Coimisiún na Scrúduithe Stáit
State Examinations Commission

Leaving Certificate Examination, 2019

HOME ECONOMICS – SCIENTIFIC AND SOCIAL

ORDINARY LEVEL

CENTRE STAMP

WEDNESDAY, 5 JUNE – AFTERNOON 2:00 to 4:30

280/320 MARKS

Instructions to Candidates

Section A   There are **twelve questions** in this section.
Answer any **ten questions**.
Each question carries **6 marks**.
Write your answers in the spaces provided on the examination paper.

Section B   There are **five questions** in this section.
Answer **Question 1 and any other two questions**.
Question 1 is worth **80 marks**.
Questions 2, 3, 4 and **5** are worth **50 marks** each.
Write your answers in the separate answer book provided.

Section C   There are **three questions** in this section.
Answer **one** elective question, to include **part (a)** and either **part (b)** or **part (c)**.

If you submitted *Textiles, Fashion and Design* coursework for examination, you may only attempt Question 2 from this section.

Electives 1 and **3** are worth **80 marks** each. **Elective 2** is worth **40 marks**.

Write your answers in the separate answer book provided.

You must return your examination paper with your answer book at the end of the examination.

Section A

Answer any **ten** questions from this section.
Each question is worth 6 marks.
Write your answers in the spaces provided.

1. Indicate with a tick (✓) whether **each** of the following statements is true or false. (6)

	True	False
Water is an essential component (part) of all body cells.		
Water helps to regulate body temperature through perspiration.		
Water prevents the digestion and absorption of food.		

2. Using the words listed below, complete the following statements in relation to vitamins. (6)

rhodopsin   *rickets*   *ascorbic acid*

A deficiency of vitamin D causes _____ in children.

Vitamin C is also known as _____ .

Vitamin A is required for the production of _____ a pigment in the retina of the eye.

3. In relation to protein explain the property: (6)

Coagulation _____

_____

_____

Name **two** different dishes that show the property of coagulation.

(i) _____   (ii) _____

4. Identify **three** changes in eating patterns in the Irish diet. (6)

(i) _____

(ii) _____

(iii) _____

5. Listed below are classes of fruit. Name **two** fruits in **each** class. (6)

Classes of Fruit	Name of Fruit
Citrus fruit	1.
	2.
Dried fruit	1.
	2.
Stone fruit	1.
	2.

6. Give **three** dietary guidelines that help prevent bowel disease. (6)

(i) _____

(ii) _____

(iii) _____

7. Name **two** different types of pastry and suggest a suitable dish that can be made using **each** type. (6)

Type of Pastry	Suitable Dish

8. Indicate with a tick (✓) whether **each** of the following statements is true or false. (6)

	True	False
Grilling is a slow method of cooking food.		
Deep frying is cooking food immersed in hot fat.		
Poaching is suitable for delicate foods e.g. eggs and fish.		

9. Using the words listed below, complete the following statements in relation to household textiles. (6)

shrink   static   proban

Fabric conditioners reduce the build-up of _____ in synthetic fibres.

Wool fabric can _____ when washed at high temperatures.

_____ is a flame-retardant finish used on household textiles.

10. What **two** factors should be considered when choosing a saving scheme? (6)

(i) _____

_____

(ii) _____

_____

Name **one** saving scheme available to consumers.

_____

11. Explain the following terms: (6)

(i) Gross Income _____

_____

(ii) Net Income _____

_____

12. What information does **each** of the following symbols convey to the consumer? (6)

_____

_____

_____

_____

_____

_____

Section B

Answer **Question 1** and any other **two questions** from this section.
Question 1 is worth 80 marks. Questions 2, 3, 4 and 5 are worth 50 marks each.

1. Bread is still considered a staple food in Ireland.

    The table below shows the types of baked goods purchased by households on a weekly basis.

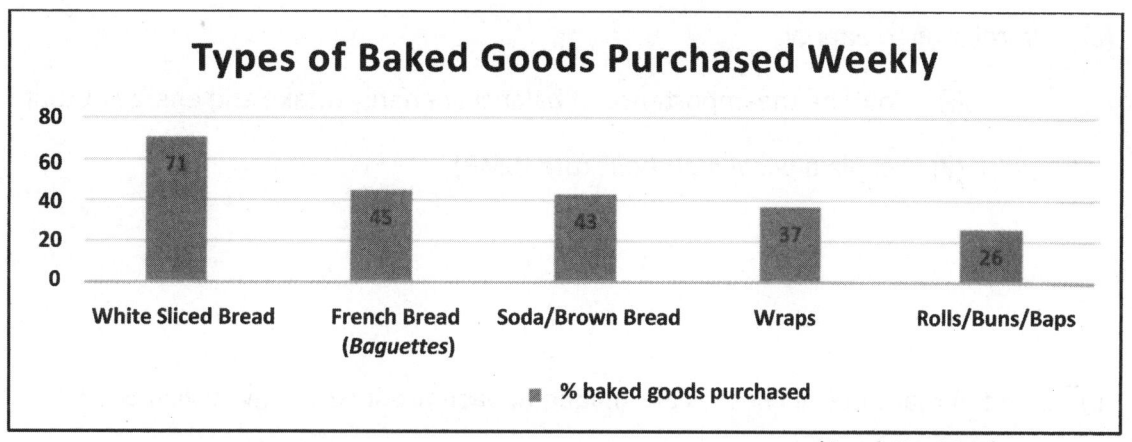

    Types of Baked Goods Purchased Weekly

Baked Good	% baked goods purchased
White Sliced Bread	71
French Bread (*Baguettes*)	45
Soda/Brown Bread	43
Wraps	37
Rolls/Buns/Baps	26

    (*Bord Bia, 2017*)

    (a) Using the information presented in the table above:

    (i) comment on **four** of the baked goods purchased weekly by households **and** give reasons for their popularity. (20)

    (ii) suggest **one** modification (change) that could be made to **one** of the baked goods to make it healthier.
    Give a reason for your choice. (5)

    (b) Give an account of carbohydrates under **each** of the following headings:
    - classification
    - dietary sources
    - functions in the body. (26)

    (c) Suggest **three** ways people can reduce sugar in their diet. (9)

    (d) Below are **four** items of consumer information found on food packaging.
    Explain the importance of **each** to the consumer:
    - additives
    - nutritional information
    - list of ingredients
    - storage instructions. (20)

2. 'Almost 1.5 billion adults around the world are not getting enough exercise.'
(Irish Times, 2018)

(a) Discuss **four** factors that determine a person's energy requirements. (20)

(b) Having regard to current healthy eating guidelines, set out a menu (3 meals) for one day for a teenager who plays sport. (18)

(c) In relation to energy:

    (i) outline the importance of balancing energy intake and energy output

    (ii) explain *basal metabolic rate* (BMR). (12)

3. 'In Ireland our farmhouse cheeses are unique to each producer.' (*www.bordbia.ie*)

(a) Give an account of **(i)** the nutritive value **and (ii)** the dietetic value of cheese. (20)

(b) Outline:

    (i) **three** different culinary uses of cheese

    (ii) the effects of heat on cheese. (18)

(c) State **three** reasons for the growing popularity of farmhouse cheeses in Ireland. (12)

4. 'Buying a house is one of the biggest financial decisions that a person can make in their lifetime.' *(www.daft.ie)*

  (a) Explain how **each** of the following would influence an individual when choosing a family home:
  - availability
  - location
  - trends in housing development. (18)

  (b) In relation to insurance:

  (i) state **three** advantages of household insurance

  (ii) outline **two** factors to be considered when choosing household insurance. (20)

  (c) Describe **three** ways to reduce pollution to promote a cleaner environment. (12)

5. 'Family plays a crucial role in modern society.' *(www.betterhelp.com)*

  (a) (i) Describe **each** of the following functions of the family:
  - economic function
  - educational function
  - physical function
  - social function.

  (ii) Explain how the state assists with **one** family function. (20)

  (b) Outline the importance of good communication within the family. (15)

  (c) Explain **three** ways of dealing with conflict between adolescents and adults. (15)

Section C

Answer **one elective question** from this section.
If you submitted *Textiles, Fashion and Design* coursework for examination,
you may **only** attempt **Question 2** from this section.

Elective 1 - Home Design and Management (80 marks)
Candidates selecting this elective must answer **1(a) and either 1(b) or 1(c)**.

1.(a) 'There are a number of ways to make buildings blend in with their environment.'

(*www.cbaarchitecture.ie*)

- **(i)** Discuss **three** environmental factors that could influence a person's choice of house style. (15)

- **(ii)** Elaborate on how **each** of the following influence house design:
    - family requirements (present and future)
    - energy efficiency
    - technological developments
    - cost. (20)

- **(iii)** List the steps to follow to obtain planning permission to build a house. (15)

and

1.(b) **(i)** Discuss **three** factors that should be considered when planning a lighting system for an open plan family kitchen/living room. (18)

(ii) Give details of **two** contemporary (modern) lighting developments suitable for a home. (12)

or

1.(c) **(i)** Name **and** describe **one** type of heating system for a new house.
Refer to:
- type of heating system
- fuel/energy source
- efficiency and convenience. (15)

(ii) Explain **three** benefits of using timers and/or thermostats in a heating system. (15)

Elective 2 - Textiles, Fashion and Design (40 marks)

Candidates selecting this elective must answer **2(a) and either 2(b) or 2(c)**.

2.(a) With so many more people taking part in leisure activities, manufacturers have become increasingly fashion conscious.

(*www.lidl.co.uk*)

- (i) Comment on the suitability of the leisure wear as shown above.
  Refer to:
    - comfort
    - aesthetic appeal
    - shape. (18)

- (ii) Sketch **and** describe a leisure wear jacket to complement the outfits. (7)

and

2.(b) Write a profile of a fabric made from manufactured fibres under the following headings:
  - fibre production
  - properties
  - fabric construction technique. (15)

or

2.(c) 'Sales of patterns for both sewing and knitting have soared by 60% in recent years.'
(*www.the guardian.co.uk*)

- (i) Discuss **three** points to be considered when selecting commercial patterns. (9)

- (ii) Explain the importance of **one** item of information found on a commercial pattern envelope. (6)

Elective 3 - Social Studies (80 marks)

Candidates selecting this elective must answer **3(a)** and either **3(b)** or **3(c)**.

3.(a) 'The numbers enrolled in higher education have been steadily increasing in recent years.'
(*www.education.ie*)

    (i) Explain *adult* and *second-chance education*. (6)

    (ii) Discuss **four** reasons for the increase in the number of students availing of third level education. (16)

    (iii) Outline **four** ways education prepares a young person for work. (16)

    (iv) How does the Protection of Young Persons (Employment) Act, 1996 protect the rights of young workers? (12)

and

3.(b) Shorter working hours have resulted in increased leisure time.

    (i) Outline **three** benefits to the family of having more leisure time. (15)

    (ii) Discuss how leisure activities help the development of the individual.
Refer to:
- physical development
- social development
- emotional development. (15)

or

3.(c) 'In Ireland today 780,000 people are living in poverty, a quarter of a million of whom are children.' (*Social Justice Ireland, 2018*)

    (i) Outline **three** reasons why poverty continues to be a feature of Irish society. (15)

    (ii) Name **and** give details of **one** voluntary organisation that helps families who are experiencing poverty. (15)

Write your Examination Number here   2018. M47

Coimisiún na Scrúduithe Stáit
State Examinations Commission

Leaving Certificate Examination, 2018

HOME ECONOMICS – SCIENTIFIC AND SOCIAL

ORDINARY LEVEL

CENTRE STAMP

WEDNESDAY, 6 JUNE – AFTERNOON 2:00 to 4:30

280/320 MARKS

Instructions to Candidates

Section A   There are **twelve questions** in this section.
Answer any **ten questions**.
Each question carries **6 marks**.
Write your answers in the spaces provided on the examination paper.

Section B   There are **five questions** in this section.
Answer **Question 1 and any other two questions**.
Question 1 is worth **80 marks**.
Questions 2, 3, 4 and **5** are worth **50 marks** each.
Write your answers in the separate answer book provided.

Section C   There are **three questions** in this section.
Answer **one** elective question, to include **part (a)** and either **part (b)** or **part (c)**.

If you submitted *Textiles, Fashion and Design* coursework for examination, you may only attempt Question 2 from this section.

Electives 1 and **3** are worth **80 marks** each. **Elective 2** is worth **40 marks**.

Write your answers in the separate answer book provided.

You must return your examination paper with your answer book at the end of the examination.

Section A

Answer any **ten** questions from this section.
Each question is worth 6 marks.
Write your answers in the spaces provided.

1. Indicate with a tick (✓) whether **each** of the following statements is true or false. (6)

	True	False
Iron is essential for the manufacture of haemoglobin in the blood.		
Anaemia is caused by lack of iron in the diet.		
A diet rich in fibre assists the absorption of iron.		

2. Using the words listed below, complete the following statements in relation to vitamins. (6)

   vitamin B   *folic acid*   *vitamin K*

   The primary function of _____ is to assist blood clotting.

   _____ is necessary for the release of energy from carbohydrate and fat.

   Neural tube defects in the unborn baby may be prevented by pregnant women

   taking _____.

3. Outline **two** ways finance (money available) affects food choices among Irish consumers. (6)

   (i) _____

   _____

   (ii) _____

   _____

4. Match **each** of the sources of lipids (fats) listed below with the correct food. (6)

animal   *marine*   *vegetable* (*plant*)

Food	Source of Lipids
Salmon	
Olive Oil	
Butter	

5. Identify **three** health problems that are caused by a diet high in sugar. (6)

(i) _____

(ii) _____

(iii) _____

6. Explain why **each** of the following is important in safe food preparation and cooking: (6)

Food storage _____

_____

Personal hygiene _____

_____

Reheating procedures _____

_____

7. Indicate with a tick (✓) whether **each** of the following statements is true or false. (6)

	True	False
Sugar is used as a preservative when making jam.		
Quick freezing results in the formation of large ice crystals within the food cell.		
Chutney is made by boiling fruit and / or vegetables with sugar, vinegar and spices.		

8. Using the words listed below, complete the following statements in relation to food spoilage and food production. (6)

        bacteria   *yeast*   *enzymes*

Cheese and yoghurt are produced using _____.

_____ cause food spoilage in fruit and vegetables.

The biological raising agent used in bread making is _____.

9. Outline **three** steps that should be followed when planning a household budget. (6)

(i) _____

_____

(ii) _____

_____

(iii) _____

_____

10. Give **one** advantage and **one** disadvantage of buying goods on credit. (6)

Advantage _____

_____

Disadvantage _____

_____

Name **two** types of credit available to consumers when buying a car.

(i) _____ (ii) _____

11. Explain **each** of the textile care symbols shown below. (6)

[iron with three dots] _____

_____

[square with three vertical lines] _____

_____

12. State **three** ways technology has contributed to greater efficiency in the home. (6)

(i) _____

_____

(ii) _____

_____

(iii) _____

_____

Section B

Answer **Question 1** and any other **two questions** from this section.
Question 1 is worth 80 marks. Questions 2, 3, 4 and 5 are worth 50 marks each.

1. Dietary protein is one of the essential nutrients that we must eat every day.

   The table below shows the ingredients and nutritional information (per 100 g), of a pre-prepared Beef Lasagne.

Pre-prepared Beef Lasagne	
Ingredients	**Nutritional Information (per 100 g)**
Chopped tomatoes, beef mince, lasagne sheets, milk, cheese, butter, tomato purée, water, onion, carrot, garlic, celery, sugar, olive oil, salt, pepper, beef stock, basil.	Energy 121 kcal Protein 6.8 g Fats 5.1 g Carbohydrate 12.6 g of which sugars 3.1 g Fibre 1.0 g Salt 0.5 g

   (a) (i) Using the information presented in the table above and having regard to current healthy eating guidelines, evaluate the nutritional value of the pre-prepared beef lasagne. (20)

   (ii) Suggest **one** suitable accompaniment that could be served with beef lasagne. Give a reason for your choice. (5)

   (b) Give an account of protein under **each** of the following headings:
   - classification
   - dietary sources
   - functions in the body. (26)

   (c) Outline **three** effects of heat on protein foods. (9)

   (d) Shopping online for food has become very popular.

   Discuss **two** advantages **and two** disadvantages of shopping online for groceries (food items). (20)

2. 'At present it is estimated that 300,000 people in Ireland have osteoporosis.'

(www.irishosteoporosis.ie)

(a) Discuss:

    (i) the causes of osteoporosis

    (ii) the effects of osteoporosis on the body. (20)

(b) Having regard to current healthy eating guidelines, set out a menu (3 meals) for one day for a person with osteoporosis. (18)

(c) Give details of **three** dietary and / or lifestyle changes that will help prevent osteoporosis. (12)

3. Cereals are the staple food of many countries.

(a) Give an account of **(i)** the nutritive value **and (ii)** the dietetic value of cereals. (20)

(b) List **three** cereals.
Name a different product made from **each** of the cereals listed. (12)

(c) In relation to cereals:

    (i) explain the difference between white (plain / cream) flour **and** wholemeal flour

    (ii) outline **three** guidelines to consider when storing cereal products. (18)

4. Seán and Áine bought a television in a sale. When they unpacked the television, they found the screen was broken. They returned the television to the shop and were refused a refund.

   (a) In your opinion, was the shop entitled to refuse a refund to Seán and Áine?
   Give reasons for your answer. (15)

   (b) (i) Name **one** reliable source of consumer advice available to Seán and Áine.

   (ii) Outline the procedure for making a complaint when a problem occurs. (20)

   (c) Explain **three** benefits of the Small Claims Court to the consumer. (15)

5. Each family member has many roles and responsibilities within the family.

   (a) Discuss **four** ways older people (grandparent/s) provide support for other members of the family. (20)

   (b) Describe **three** ways older people can maintain (keep) their independence. (15)

   (c) Explain *generation conflict*.
   Outline **two** ways of dealing with generation conflict. (15)

Section C

Answer **one elective question** from this section.
If you submitted *Textiles, Fashion and Design* coursework for examination,
you may **only** attempt **Question 2** from this section.

Elective 1 - Home Design and Management (80 marks)
Candidates selecting this elective must answer **1(a)** and either **1(b)** or **1(c)**.

1.(a) 'We value water as a precious natural resource on which the quality of life depends.'

(*www.engineersireland.ie*)

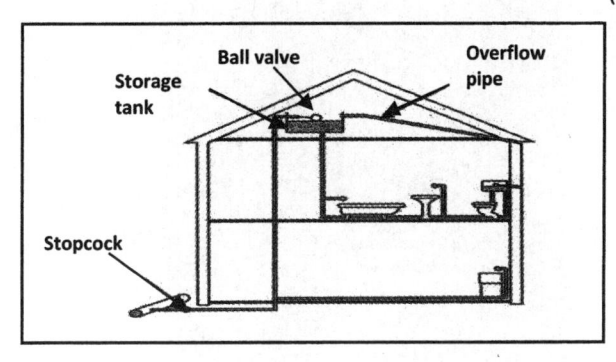

    (i) Explain the function of the following parts of the cold-water system shown above:

- stopcock
- ball valve (ballcock)
- overflow pipe. (18)

    (ii) Describe **each** of the following stages in the water treatment process:

      (a) screening   **(b)** chlorination   **(c)** fluoridation   **(d)** testing. (16)

    (iii) Outline **four** ways of conserving water in the home. (16)

and

1.(b) Proximity to local amenities can add value to a house.

    (i) Discuss the benefits of **three** local amenities for families with young children. (15)

    (ii) Give **three** reasons why renting a house is a more popular choice than buying for some people. (15)

or

1.(c) **(i)** Outline **three** factors that a student should consider when selecting furniture for a bedroom. (15)

    (ii) Identify **and** describe **three** items of storage furniture suitable for a student's rented accommodation. (15)

Elective 2 - Textiles, Fashion and Design (40 marks)

Candidates selecting this elective must answer **2(a) and either 2(b) or 2(c)**.

2.(a) 'A school uniform can play a crucial role in establishing and maintaining the school identity.'

(www.oireachtas.ie)

(www.aldi.ie)

- (i) Comment on the suitability of the uniforms as shown above for primary school students. Refer to:
  - function
  - comfort
  - aesthetic appeal. (18)

- (ii) Suggest **two** methods that could be used to apply a crest to the uniform. (7)

and

2.(b) Modern fabrics have a variety of finishes applied to them during manufacture.

- (i) Explain why fabric finishes are used on fabric. (9)

- (ii) Name **and** describe **one** fabric finish. (6)

or

2.(c) 'A new season means new fashion.' (www.stellar.ie)

- (i) Outline **three** factors that influence fashion changes. (9)

- (ii) Describe **two** challenges (difficulties) affecting the growth of the Irish clothing industry. (6)

Elective 3 - Social Studies (80 marks)

Candidates selecting this elective must answer **3(a) and either 3(b) or 3(c)**.

3.(a) 'Youth unemployment across Europe remains far too high.'   (*Irish Examiner, 2017*)

    (i) Define *unemployment*. (6)

    (ii) Outline the effects of unemployment on:
- the young adult
- the family
- society. (24)

    (iii) Discuss the importance of an educational qualification for young people. (8)

    (iv) Name **and** give details of **one** programme / course designed to train and upskill the unemployed. (12)

and

3.(b) 'Empowering women in the workplace is a win-win for us all.'   (*Irish Independent, 2017*)

    (i) Explain **three** reasons why there is an increase in the number of women in the workplace. (15)

    (ii) Outline the advantages **and** the disadvantages for family life of dual-earners (both parents working). (15)

or

3.(c) 'Almost two-thirds of the population are now living in urban areas.'
   (*The Irish Times, 2017*)

    (i) Discuss **three** reasons why more people live in urban areas. (15)

    (ii) Explain **three** ways that migration (moving) from rural to urban areas has impacted on life in rural areas. (15)

Write your Examination Number here [ ] 2017. M47

Coimisiún na Scrúduithe Stáit
State Examinations Commission

Leaving Certificate Examination, 2017

HOME ECONOMICS – SCIENTIFIC AND SOCIAL

ORDINARY LEVEL

CENTRE STAMP

WEDNESDAY, 7 JUNE – AFTERNOON, 2.00 to 4.30

280/320 MARKS

Instructions to Candidates

Section A   There are **twelve** questions in this section.
Candidates are required to answer any **ten** questions.
Each question carries **6** marks.
Write your answers in the spaces provided on the examination paper.

Section B   There are **five** questions in this section.
Candidates are required to answer **Question 1 and any other two questions**.
Question 1 is worth **80** marks.
Questions 2, 3, 4 and 5 are worth **50** marks each.
Write your answers in the separate answer book provided.

Section C   There are **three** questions in this section.
Candidates are required to answer **one** elective question to include
part **(a)** and either part **(b)** or part **(c)**.
Candidates who submitted Textiles, Fashion and Design coursework for examination may only attempt Elective Question 2 from this section.
Electives **1** and **3** are worth **80** marks each. Elective **2** is worth **40** marks.
Write your answers in the separate answer book provided.

You must return your examination paper with your answer book at the end of the examination.

Section A

Answer any **ten** questions from this section.
Each question is worth 6 marks.
Write your answers in the spaces provided.

1. Indicate with a tick (✓) whether **each** of the following statements is true or false. (6)

	True	False
Lipids (fats) are made up of fatty acids and glycerol.		
Lipids (fats) contain the element nitrogen.		
Omega 3 fatty acids help reduce the risk of heart disease.		

2. Name **three** different sources of fibre in the diet. (6)

   (i) _____

   (ii) _____

   (iii) _____

3. Indicate with a tick (✓) which of the protein foods listed below are of high biological value and which are of low biological value. (6)

Protein Foods	High Biological Value	Low Biological Value
Eggs		
Peas		
Fish		

4. List **two** biological functions of calcium. (6)

   (i) _____

   (ii) _____

   Name **two** good dietary sources of calcium.

   (i) _____ (ii) _____

5. Outline **three** healthy eating guidelines for pregnant women. (6)

   (i) _____

   (ii) _____

   (iii) _____

6. Give **two** examples of different foods suitable for **each** of the following methods of cooking. (6)

Methods of Cooking	Example 1	Example 2
Grilling		
Steaming		
Roasting		

7. Using the words listed below, complete the following statements in relation to cereals. (6)

   bran   endosperm   staple

   The largest part of the grain is the _____ which contains the starch.

   Cereals are _____ foods in many countries.

   The _____ layer is composed mainly of cellulose.

298

8. Indicate with a tick (✓) whether **each** of the following statements is true or false. (6)

	True	False
Food additives prolong (increase) the shelf life of foods.		
Artificial colourings are permitted in baby food.		
The use of food additives is regulated by EU legislation.		

9. State **three** ways the *Sale of Goods and Supply of Services Act (1980)* protects the consumer. (6)

(i) _____

_____

(ii) _____

_____

(iii) _____

_____

10. Outline **two** points to be considered when selecting textiles for the home. (6)

(i) _____

(ii) _____

Name **two** fabrics suitable for household textiles.

(i) _____ (ii) _____

11. Explain **one** benefit of the label below to the consumer. (6)

[Energy label for Fridge-Freezer, rated A, Energy consumption 325 kWh/year, Fresh food volume 190 l, Frozen food volume 126 l]

(www.which.co.uk)

12. Give **one** example of the following types of pollution. (6)

Types of pollution	Example
Air pollution	
Water pollution	
Noise pollution	

300

Section B

Answer **Question 1** and any other **two** questions from this section.
Question 1 is worth 80 marks. Questions 2, 3, 4 and 5 are worth 50 marks each.

1. **'The World Health Organisation recommends the consumption of at least five portions of fruit or vegetables daily.'** *(Healthy Ireland Survey, 2015)*

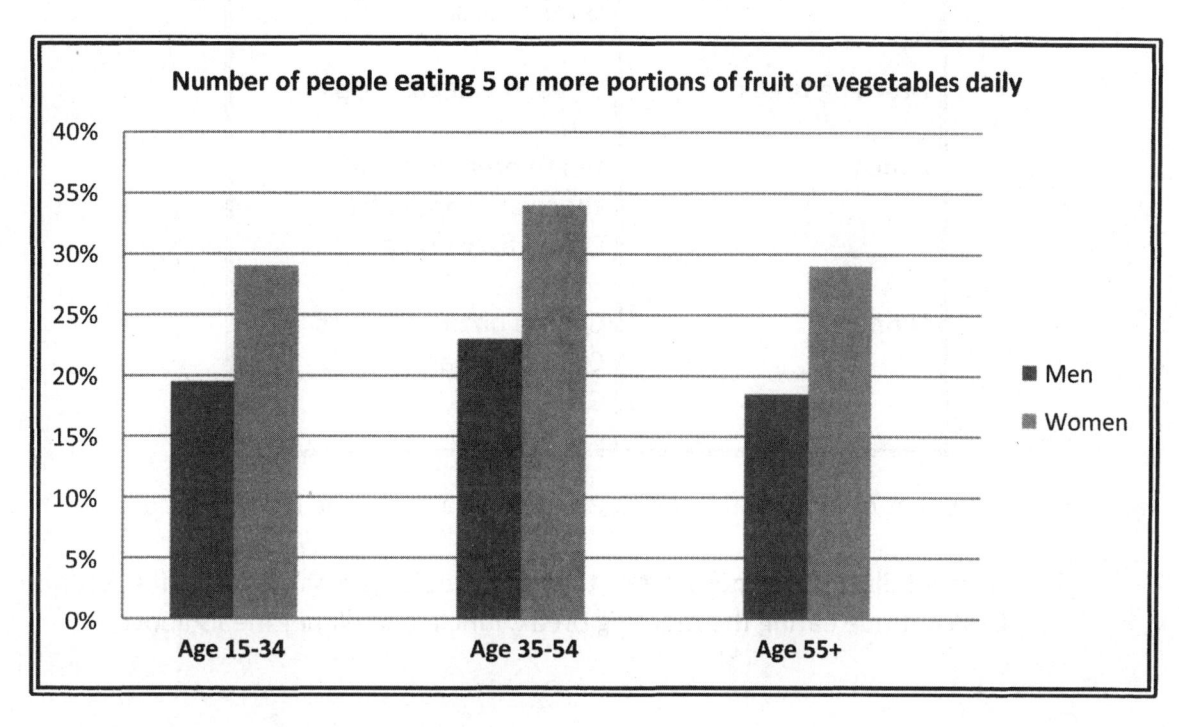

Number of people eating 5 or more portions of fruit or vegetables daily

(Bar chart showing percentages for Men and Women across three age groups:
- Age 15-34: Men ~19%, Women ~29%
- Age 35-54: Men ~23%, Women ~34%
- Age 55+: Men ~18%, Women ~29%)

(a) Using the information provided above:

   (i) comment on the table **and** give **one** reason why women consume (eat) more fruit and vegetables than men in **each** of the **three** different age groups. (15)

   (ii) suggest **three** ways that men can increase their daily intake of fruit and vegetables. (12)

(b) Give an account of Vitamin C under **each** of the following headings:

   - dietary sources
   - functions in the body
   - effect of deficiency. (28)

(c) Vitamin C assists the absorption of nutrients. Name **one** of these nutrients. (5)

(d) Discuss **four** factors to be considered by consumers when selecting **and** buying pre-prepared (convenience) fruit and vegetables. (20)

2. A breakfast club is a chance for students to have their most important meal of the day. Paul and Lisa attend a breakfast club in their post-primary school. The table below shows the meals eaten by Paul and Lisa on a typical school day.

Breakfast (Breakfast Club)	Bowl of porridge Carton of yoghurt Glass of orange juice
Morning break	Salt and vinegar crisps
Lunch	White bread roll with chocolate spread filling Can of fizzy orange
Dinner	Cheese pizza and chips Chocolate bar Glass of milk

(a) (i) Comment on the breakfast that Paul and Lisa eat at the breakfast club.

    (ii) Give details of **three** possible diet related problems that may arise if Paul and Lisa continue eating the morning break, lunch, and dinner meals above. (20)

(b) Suggest an alternative menu for Paul and Lisa's morning break, lunch **and** dinner. (15)

(c) Discuss **three** factors that affect the food choices of students in post-primary school. (15)

3. 'Your Craft Butcher respects meat as a quality product and will happily provide cookery tips and storage advice to customers.' (www.craftbutchers.ie)

(a) Give an account of **(i)** the nutritive value **and (ii)** the dietetic value of meat. (20)

(b) Outline:
    (i) the effects of cooking on meat
    (ii) the guidelines for storing meat. (16)

(c) Explain **two** causes of toughness in meat **and** name **two** different methods of tenderising meat. (14)

4. **Refrigerators are designed to keep food fresh and assist in reducing food waste.**

   (a) Discuss **four** factors that should be considered when selecting a refrigerator for a family. (20)

   (b) Set out the results of a study you have carried out on a refrigeration appliance. Refer to:
   - type of refrigeration appliance
   - guidelines for use
   - modern features. (20)

   (c) Outline **two** sources of consumer information available to consumers when purchasing household appliances. (10)

5. **The family is one of the most important institutions in our society, and has been subject to rapid and fundamental change.**

   (a) Describe **each** of the following family structures:
   - nuclear family
   - extended family
   - blended family. (18)

   (b) Discuss **three** ways in which gender roles have changed in the modern family. (15)

   (c) Give **one** reason why it is important to make a will.
   Outline **three** important features of a valid will. (17)

Section C

Answer **one elective question** from this section.
Candidates who submitted Textiles, Fashion and Design coursework for examination may only attempt elective question 2.

Elective 1 – Home Design and Management (80 marks)

Candidates selecting this elective must answer **1(a)** and either **1(b)** or **1(c)**.

1.(a) **Examples of housing styles in Ireland are shown below.**

(www.google.com)   (www.plan-a-home.ie)   (www.seandaly.com)

(i) Discuss **four** factors that may influence a young couple's choice of housing style. (20)

(ii) Name **and** describe **one** method of insulation you would recommend for **each** of the following areas in a house:

- attic
- walls
- windows. (15)

(iii) State **three** advantages of having a house well insulated. (15)

and

1.(b) **Colour is a powerful tool used in design to create a beautiful home.**

(i) Explain how colour can be used to create atmosphere in a family home. (15)

(ii) Suggest **two** soft furnishings that would enhance the appearance of a newly decorated living room. Give reasons for your choice. (15)

or

1.(c) **'Electricity is a powerful and versatile energy but can be dangerous if it is not used properly.'** (www.esbnetworks.ie)

(i) Outline **three** guidelines for the safe use of electricity in the home. (15)

(ii) Recommend **one** type of energy supply (other than electricity) to the home. Give reasons for your choice. (15)

Elective 2 - Textiles, Fashion and Design (40 marks)

Candidates selecting this elective must answer **2(a) and either 2(b) or 2(c)**.

2.(a) **The Debs (graduation) is a very important occasion in many teenagers lives.**

(www.debs-suits-online.com)   (www.debs-dresses-online.com)

    (i) Comment on the suitability of the debs (graduation) outfits as shown above. Refer to:

- shape
- proportion
- design features. (18)

    (ii) Suggest **one** accessory you could add to enhance either of the above outfits. Give a reason for your choice. (7)

and

2.(b) **'Natural fibres are fashionable and the fibre of choice for many young designers.'**
(www.wildfibres.co.uk)

    (i) Classify natural fibres **and** give **one** example in **each** class. (8)

    (ii) Name **and** describe **one** test to identify a natural fibre. (7)

or

2.(c) **Fashion designers have made fashion a huge industry in the 21st century.**

    (i) Name **one** Irish fashion designer **and** comment on his / her contribution to Irish fashion. (6)

    (ii) Outline **three** fashion trends currently popular with teenagers. (9)

Elective 3 - Social Studies (80 marks)

Candidates selecting this elective must answer **3(a)** and either **3(b)** or **3(c)**.

3.(a) **'Since the onset of the recession the number of people in poverty in Ireland has increased by more than 100,000. Today there are more than 750,000 people living in poverty in Ireland.'** *(www.socialjustice.ie 2016)*

    (i) Define *poverty*. (6)

        Explain **each** of the following:
- relative poverty
- absolute poverty. (12)

    (ii) Name **three** groups of people at risk of poverty **and** state the effect of poverty on **each** group. (18)

    (iii) Name **and** give details of **one** voluntary organisation that provides support to people at risk of poverty. (14)

and

3.(b) Work fills a large part of a person's life.

    (i) Discuss **three** factors that affect a person's attitude to their work. (15)

    (ii) Outline the benefits of voluntary work to:
- the individual
- the community. (15)

or

3.(c) **'Early childhood is a really important and exciting phase of a child's life, when they learn so much about themselves, others, and the world around them.'** *(www.limerickchildcare.ie)*

    (i) Name **and** give details of **two** pre-school options available to parents for their children. (15)

    (ii) Discuss **three** advantages of attending pre-school for young children. (15)

Write your Examination Number here [   ]   2016. M47

Coimisiún na Scrúduithe Stáit
State Examinations Commission

Leaving Certificate Examination, 2016

HOME ECONOMICS – SCIENTIFIC AND SOCIAL

ORDINARY LEVEL

CENTRE STAMP

WEDNESDAY, 8 JUNE – AFTERNOON, 2.00 to 4.30

280/320 MARKS

Instructions to Candidates

Section A There are **twelve** questions in this section.
Candidates are required to answer any **ten** questions.
Each question carries **6** marks.
Write your answers in the spaces provided on the examination paper.

Section B There are **five** questions in this section.
Candidates are required to answer **Question 1 and any other two questions**.
Question 1 is worth **80** marks.
Questions 2, 3, 4 and 5 are worth **50** marks each.
Write your answers in the separate answer book provided.

Section C There are **three** questions in this section.
Candidates are required to answer **one** elective question to include
part (a) and either **part (b)** or **part (c)**.
Candidates who submitted Textiles, Fashion and Design coursework for examination may attempt only Question 2 from this section.
Electives **1** and **3** are worth **80** marks each. Elective **2** is worth **40** marks.
Write your answers in the separate answer book provided.

You must return your examination paper with your answer book at the end of the examination.

Section A

Answer any <u>ten</u> questions from this section.
Each question is worth 6 marks.
Write your answers in the spaces provided.

1. Indicate with a tick (✓) whether **each** of the following statements is true or false. (6)

	True	False
Protein is the only nutrient that contains nitrogen.		
Excess protein is stored as adipose tissue.		
Protein is necessary for the growth of body cells.		

2. Give **one** dietary source of **each** of the following carbohydrates. (6)

Carbohydrate	Dietary source
Sugar	
Starch	
Fibre	

3. State **two** functions of Vitamin A. (6)

   (i) _____

   (ii) _____

   Name **two** good dietary sources of Vitamin A.

   (i) _____ (ii) _____

4. List **three** factors that influence the energy requirements of teenagers. (6)

   (i) _____

   (ii) _____

   (iii) _____

308

5. Name **two** nutrients necessary in the diet to prevent osteoporosis. (6)

(i) _____ (ii) _____

State **one** lifestyle change that would improve bone health.

_____

6. Using the words listed below, complete the following statements in relation to cheese. (6)

curds, lactic acid, rennin

In the production of cheese a culture is added to milk to convert the lactose to

_____ . The enzyme _____ changes caseinogen to

casein. The mixture is allowed to rest for 30 minutes and separates into _____

and whey.

7. Indicate with a tick (✓) whether **each** of the following statements is true or false. (6)

	True	False
Quick freezing at -25°C forms small ice crystals within the food cells.		
Bananas and lettuce are suitable foods for freezing.		
Vegetables are blanched before freezing to destroy enzymes.		

8. Give **two** examples of vegetables in **each** of the following classes. (6)

Classes	Example 1	Example 2
Pulse vegetables		
Root vegetables		
Green vegetables		

9. Explain the term *gross pay*. (6)

_____

_____

Name **two** compulsory deductions taken from gross pay.

(i) _____ (ii) _____

10. What information does **each** of the following fabric care symbols convey to the consumer? (6)

_____

_____

_____

_____

11. Indicate with a tick (✓) which of the following household appliances has a motor **or** an element.
(6)

Household appliance	Element	Motor
Kettle		
Food processor		
Toaster		

12. Name **two** sources of renewable energy. (6)

(i) _____ (ii) _____

Explain the benefit of renewable energy to the environment.

_____

_____

_____

Section B

Answer Question 1 and any other two questions from this section.
Question 1 is worth 80 marks. Questions 2, 3, 4 and 5 are worth 50 marks each.

1. 'Saturated fat has a bad reputation in recent years, but it might not be entirely deserved. Foods such as milk that are high in SFA (saturated fatty acids) **and high in calcium don't seem to raise harmful cholesterol levels.**' *(Paula Mee, The Irish Times, July 2015)*

    The table below shows the nutritional content of two pre-prepared meals.

Pre-prepared meal	Ingredients	Nutritional Information (per serving)	
Fisherman's pie	Potato, cod, cream, milk, butter, cheese, onion, peas, salt.	Energy Fat Carbohydrates Fibre Protein Salt	392 kcal 18.4 g 37.9 g 3.1 g 17.2 g 1.9 g
Chicken curry with rice	White rice, chicken, apple, onion, curry powder, garlic, tomato puree, flour, salt.	Energy Fat Carbohydrates Fibre Protein Salt	524 kcal 8.0 g 88.0 g 4.8 g 22.0 g 1.7 g

    (a) Using the information presented in the table above, state which of the pre-prepared meals you would recommend for a young person involved in sport. Explain **three** reasons for your choice. (20)

    (b) Give an account of lipids (fats) under **each** of the following headings:

    - classification
    - functions in the body
    - dietary sources. (28)

    (c) Outline **three** ways an individual can reduce his / her intake of fat. (12)

    (d) Discuss **four** ways consumers can be environmentally aware when shopping and buying food for family meals. (20)

2. 'Going vegetarian is one of the best things you could do for your health. All the nutrients you need are easily provided in a vegetarian diet.' *(Vegetarian Society of Ireland, July 2015)*

    (a) Discuss **four** reasons why some teenagers become vegetarian. (20)

    (b) Having regard to current healthy eating guidelines, set out a menu (3 meals) for one day for a lacto-vegetarian to ensure their nutritional needs are met. (18)

    (c) Explain **three** guidelines that should be followed when preparing **and** cooking vegetables to retain maximum nutrients. (12)

3. 'Eggs are great value, easy to cook and a very versatile ingredient for both savoury and sweet dishes.' *(www.bordbia.ie)*

    (a) Describe **(i)** the nutritional **and (ii)** the dietetic value of eggs. (20)

    (b) Outline:
        (i) the factors to be considered when storing eggs
        (ii) the effects of heat on eggs. (20)

    (c) Describe **two** items of consumer information found on an egg carton (box). (10)

4. Saoirse is a 1st year college student living away from home and sharing a house with two other students. She has a weekly allowance of €220, for all her college expenses including rent, and she cycles to college.

(a) Discuss **four** reasons why Saoirse should set out a budget. (20)

(b) Set out a weekly budget plan showing how Saoirse should allocate her money to ensure her needs and wants are met. (20)

(c) Suggest **one** suitable savings account that you would recommend for Saoirse. Give **one** reason for your choice. (10)

5. 'According to the Annual Report of the Registrar General for 2014, some 22,033 marriages were recorded for the year, a 6.6% increase over the figure in 2013.'
(Irish Independent, July 2015)

(a) Discuss why marriage is a popular option for couples in Ireland today. (15)

(b) Discuss **(i)** the rights **and (ii)** the responsibilities of a couple within the marriage relationship. (20)

(c) Name **and** give an account of **one** option available to couples who are experiencing difficulties in their marriage. (15)

Section C

Answer **one** question from this section.
Candidates who submitted Textiles, Fashion and Design coursework for examination may attempt **only** Question 2.

Elective 1 – Home Design and Management (80 marks)

Candidates selecting this elective must answer 1(a) and either 1(b) **or** 1(c).

1.(a) Kitchen design requires careful consideration and planning.
The diagram shows the layout of a kitchen.

(www.buzhomedesign.com)

- (i) Evaluate the suitability of the kitchen for a couple with two young children under **each** of the following headings:

    - suitability for family use
    - ventilation
    - ergonomics (work triangle). (20)

- (ii) Discuss **three** factors which should be considered when choosing heating for the kitchen. (15)

- (iii) Suggest **three** ways to improve the energy efficiency of a kitchen. (15)

and

1.(b) The floor makes up a large part of the surface area of any room and thus has a definite effect on the overall appearance of the room.

- (i) Give an account of **four** factors that should be considered when choosing floor coverings for a family home. (20)

- (ii) Suggest **one** type of floor covering suitable for a family bathroom.
State **two** properties of the selected floor covering. (10)

or

1.(c) Today less people can afford to buy their own home.

- (i) Explain why the cost of rental accommodation has increased in urban areas. (12)

- (ii) Name a suitable type of accommodation for **each** of the following people:

    (a) a college student **(b)** a person with reduced mobility **and** **(c)** an elderly couple.

    Give **one** reason for your choice in **each** case. (18)

Elective 2 - Textiles, Fashion and Design (40 marks)

Candidates selecting this elective must answer 2(a) and either 2(b) **or** 2(c).

2.(a) Nothing can quite prepare you for the experience of your first office job.

(www.pinterest.com)

(i) Comment on the suitability of the office suits as shown above.
Refer to:
- function
- comfort
- aesthetic appeal. (18)

(ii) Suggest **one** fabric suitable for the suit jacket **and** give a reason for your choice. (7)

and

2.(b) Natural fabrics have many advantages over synthetic fabrics.

(i) Write a profile of a natural fabric under **each** of the following headings:
- fibre production
- how the fabric is constructed. (9)

(ii) Give **two** advantages of using natural fibres / fabric in clothing. (6)

or

2.(c) 'I love fashion. I think it's so important because it's how you show yourself to the world.' *(Emma Watson, April 2015)*

(i) Explain how the media influences the choice of clothing worn by teenagers. (9)

(ii) Discuss the contribution of modern footwear to current fashion trends. (6)

Elective 3 - Social Studies (80 marks)

Candidates selecting this elective must answer 3(a) and either 3(b) or 3(c).

3.(a) Work has a direct impact on resources such as time and money, and affects the amount of each available for family life.

    (i) Explain **each** of the following:

- paid work
- unpaid work
- voluntary work. (18)

    (ii) Discuss the advantages **and** the disadvantage of students working in part-time employment. (20)

    (iii) How does the Protection of Young Persons (Employment) Act, 1996 protect young people in the labour force? (12)

and

3.(b) Recently, third level colleges have seen a big increase in the number of mature students applying for places on courses.

    (i) Discuss **three** reasons why adults are returning to education. (18)

    (ii) Name **and** give details of **one** initiative available to adults to improve their educational qualifications. (12)

or

3.(c) Many people are stressed by life, this is why leisure activities are crucial to the development of a good work / life balance.

    (i) Define *leisure*. (6)

    (ii) Describe how family leisure activities are influenced by **each** of the following:

- age
- occupation
- culture
- cost. (24)

LOL

SAY NO TO BULLYING
NOBODY DESERVES TO BE BULLIED
TELL AN ADULT YOU CAN TRUST

This Anti-Bullying campaign is supported by the Department of Education and Skills with the co-operation of the Irish Educational Publishers Association

Edco 2024/2025 School Year Planner

KEY DATES

- ● Public Holidays
- ■ School Holidays
- ♦ Important Dates

October 2024 mid-term break: All schools will close from Monday 28th October 2024 to 1st November 2024 inclusive.

Christmas 2024: All schools will close on Friday 20th December 2024, which will be the final day of the school term. All schools will re-open on Monday 6th January 2025.

February 2025 mid-term break: Post-Primary schools will close from Monday 17th February to Friday 21st February 2025 inclusive.

Easter 2025: All schools will close on Friday 11th April 2025 which will be the final day of the school term. All schools will re-open on Monday 28th April 2025.

5th November – CAO application facility opens for 2025 applications

1st February – Normal closing date for CAO applications

1st May – Closing date for late CAO applications

1st July – Change Your Mind CAO Deadline

The start date for the Junior & Leaving Certificate Examinations 2025 will be Wednesday 4th June.

SEPTEMBER	OCTOBER	NOVEMBER	DECEMBER	JANUARY	FEBRUARY	MARCH	APRIL	MAY	JUNE	JULY	AUGUST
1 Sun	1 Tues	1 Fri ■	1 Sun	1 Wed	1 Sat ♦	1 Sat	1 Tues	1 Thurs ♦	1 Sun	1 Tues ♦	1 Fri
2 Mon	2 Wed	2 Sat	2 Mon	2 Thurs ●	2 Sun	2 Sun	2 Wed	2 Fri	2 Mon ●	2 Wed	2 Sat
3 Tues	3 Thurs	3 Sun	3 Tues	3 Fri	3 Mon ●	3 Mon	3 Thurs	3 Sat	3 Tues	3 Thurs	3 Sun
4 Wed	4 Fri	4 Mon	4 Wed	4 Sat	4 Tues	4 Tues	4 Fri	4 Sun	4 Wed ♦	4 Fri	4 Mon ●
5 Thurs	5 Sat	5 Tues ♦	5 Thurs	5 Sun	5 Wed	5 Wed	5 Sat	5 Mon ●	5 Thurs	5 Sat	5 Tues
6 Fri	6 Sun	6 Wed	6 Fri	6 Mon	6 Thurs	6 Thurs	6 Sun	6 Tues	6 Fri	6 Sun	6 Wed
7 Sat	7 Mon	7 Thurs	7 Sat	7 Tues	7 Fri	7 Fri	7 Mon	7 Wed	7 Sat	7 Mon	7 Thurs
8 Sun	8 Tues	8 Fri	8 Sun	8 Wed	8 Sat	8 Sat	8 Tues	8 Thurs	8 Sun	8 Tues	8 Fri
9 Mon	9 Wed	9 Sat	9 Mon	9 Thurs	9 Sun	9 Sun	9 Wed	9 Fri	9 Mon	9 Wed	9 Sat
10 Tues	10 Thurs	10 Sun	10 Tues	10 Fri	10 Mon	10 Mon	10 Thurs	10 Sat	10 Tues	10 Thurs	10 Sun
11 Wed	11 Fri	11 Mon	11 Wed	11 Sat	11 Tues	11 Tues	11 Fri	11 Sun	11 Wed	11 Fri	11 Mon
12 Thurs	12 Sat	12 Tues	12 Thurs	12 Sun	12 Wed	12 Wed	12 Sat	12 Mon	12 Thurs	12 Sat	12 Tues
13 Fri	13 Sun	13 Wed	13 Fri	13 Mon	13 Thurs	13 Thurs	13 Sun	13 Tues	13 Fri	13 Sun	13 Wed
14 Sat	14 Mon	14 Thurs	14 Sat	14 Tues	14 Fri	14 Fri	14 Mon ■	14 Wed	14 Sat	14 Mon	14 Thurs
15 Sun	15 Tues	15 Fri	15 Sun	15 Wed	15 Sat	15 Sat	15 Tues ■	15 Thurs	15 Sun	15 Tues	15 Fri
16 Mon	16 Wed	16 Sat	16 Mon	16 Thurs	16 Sun	16 Sun	16 Wed ■	16 Fri	16 Mon	16 Wed	16 Sat
17 Tues	17 Thurs	17 Sun	17 Tues	17 Fri	17 Mon ■	17 Mon ●	17 Thurs ■	17 Sat	17 Tues	17 Thurs	17 Sun
18 Wed	18 Fri	18 Mon	18 Wed	18 Sat	18 Tues ■	18 Tues	18 Fri ■	18 Sun	18 Wed	18 Fri	18 Mon
19 Thurs	19 Sat	19 Tues	19 Thurs	19 Sun	19 Wed ■	19 Wed	19 Sat	19 Mon	19 Thurs	19 Sat	19 Tues
20 Fri	20 Sun	20 Wed	20 Fri	20 Mon	20 Thurs ■	20 Thurs	20 Sun	20 Tues	20 Fri	20 Sun	20 Wed
21 Sat	21 Mon	21 Thurs	21 Sat	21 Tues	21 Fri ■	21 Fri	21 Mon ●	21 Wed	21 Sat	21 Mon	21 Thurs
22 Sun	22 Tues	22 Fri	22 Sun	22 Wed	22 Sat	22 Sat	22 Tues	22 Thurs	22 Sun	22 Tues	22 Fri
23 Mon	23 Wed	23 Sat	23 Mon ■	23 Thurs	23 Sun	23 Sun	23 Wed	23 Fri	23 Mon	23 Wed	23 Sat
24 Tues	24 Thurs	24 Sun	24 Tues	24 Fri	24 Mon	24 Mon	24 Thurs	24 Sat	24 Tues	24 Thurs	24 Sun
25 Wed	25 Fri	25 Mon	25 Wed ●	25 Sat	25 Tues	25 Tues	25 Fri ■	25 Sun	25 Wed	25 Fri	25 Mon
26 Thurs	26 Sat	26 Tues	26 Thurs ●	26 Sun	26 Wed	26 Wed	26 Sat	26 Mon	26 Thurs	26 Sat	26 Tues
27 Fri	27 Sun	27 Wed	27 Fri	27 Mon	27 Thurs	27 Thurs	27 Sun	27 Tues	27 Fri	27 Sun	27 Wed
28 Sat	28 Mon ●	28 Thurs	28 Sat	28 Tues	28 Fri	28 Fri	28 Mon	28 Wed	28 Sat	28 Mon	28 Thurs
29 Sun	29 Tues ■	29 Fri	29 Sun	29 Wed		29 Sat	29 Tues	29 Thurs	29 Sun	29 Tues	29 Fri
30 Mon	30 Wed ■	30 Sat	30 Mon	30 Thurs		30 Sun	30 Wed	30 Fri	30 Mon	30 Wed	30 Sat
	31 Thurs ■		31 Tues	31 Fri		31 Mon		31 Sat		31 Thurs	31 Sun

FOR FREE ONLINE SOLUTIONS

visit www.e-xamit.ie